NATIVE AMERICAN
PLACE NAMES
OF
MASSACHUSETTS

R. A. DOUGLAS-LITHGOW

APPLEWOOD BOOKS
Bedford, Massachusetts

Native American Place Names of Massachusetts was published originally in 1909 as part of *Indian Place and Proper Names of New England*.

Thank you for purchasing an Applewood Book.
Applewood reprints America's lively classics—books from the past that are still of interest to modern readers. For a free copy of our current catalog, please write to Applewood Books, P.O. Box 365, Bedford, MA 01730.

ISBN 1-55709-542-6

Library of Congress Catalog Card Number: 2001086346

10 9 8 7 6 5 4 3 2 1

CONTENTS.

PREFACE

"The names which the original inhabitants assigned to our mountains, plains and valleys, are mostly lost. Many of our rivers, bays, and falls of water are yet known by their ancient Indian names. On account of their originality, antiquity, signification, singularity, and sound, these names ought to be carefully preserved. In every respect they are far preferable to the unmeaning application, and constant repetition of an improper English name.

Samuel Williams, LL.D., *Natural and Civil History of Vermont.*
Vol. 1, p. 43. 1809.

My sole aim in the production of this volume has been to collect the accessible Native American place and proper names of Massachusetts, and to give the locations of the one, with their interpretations, as far as possible, and the tribal affiliations of the other. No attempt has been made to enter into their philological significance, and where the geographical setting of orthographical varieties of the same name presents approximate but different localities, it is because I have found them so described by different authorities. I have, moreover, culled these names from every practicable source that I could discover, so that they might be preserved for those who may take an interest in them now or hereafter.

These words represent almost all that remains of the aboriginal inhabitants of this country,— a brave, noble and patriotic race who, opposed by the overwhelming and heedless forces of civilization, did everything the bravest and noblest could do to obey the first law of Nature: self-preservation. The race has almost disappeared from our New England States, and the means used for its effacement reflect little credit upon their successors; but there are many, and an increasing number, who cherish and would keep green memories of the vanquished aborigines, and I must include myself among them.

It is really marvellous that so many of the aboriginal names are spared to us especially when we remember that the Indians had no written language,— that in the northern New England States the French missionaries and the early settlers had to reproduce as nearly as possible the spoken word by phonetic means alone, and that throughout the more southerly States, the early English settlers had only similar means at their disposal. It is scarcely, therefore, a matter for surprise that many of the original Indian words have become more or less corrupt in their formation and orthography, and that their original character has been lost by their transference from one language to another. The ignorance of scribes, and the absence of orthographical exactitude prevailing generally during the 17th century have made confusion more confounded, so that, in many cases, as Trumbull says, the words have "suffered some mutilation or change of form." Thanks, however, to the efforts of many scholarly men, some of whom were contemporary with the Indians, linguistic and dialectical difficulties have been to some extent surmounted, and in numerous instances the true character, orthographical correctness and real signification of the words have been reproduced and restored.

In a few instances place-names have been introduced which, strictly speaking, should not have been included within the scope of this volume, but, as these names constantly recur throughout the history of New England during the 17th century it has been thought advisable to retain them.

Where several forms of the same place-name are given I have wherever practicable, indicated the forms generally accepted by having them italicised.

With regard to the place-names of Conn: I have been compelled, for obvious reasons, to make free use of the late Dr. Trumbull's classical work on this subject, but, at the same time I have materially increased the number of names. Mr. S. S. Rider's admirable work on "The Lands of Rhode Island" has been simply invaluable with regard to the place-names of this State, and I hereby gratefully express my obligation.

My cordial thanks are due to Lucius C. Hubbard, Esq., the Hon. J. G. Crawford, and Hon. S. A. Green, M. D., LL. D. for permission to select from or reproduce Indian words and place-names contained in their respective works; also to the Librarians of the several New England Historical Societies for ever-ready and highly esteemed assistance.

To the courteous Librarian of the Boston Public Library, Horace G. Wadlin, Esq., and his efficient staff, especially to Miss Agnes Doyle, and Mr. Blaisdell,— I am deeply indebted for never-failing kindness in their respective departments; and also to W. Prescott Greenlaw, Esq., Librarian of the New England Historic Genealogical Society.

To Otis G. Hammond, Esq., M. A., Assistant Editor of the State Papers, at the State Library, Concord, N. H., I owe a special debt of gratitude for valuable cooperation cordially and generously rendered; also to H. A. Wright, Esq., of Springfield, Mass., author of "Indian Deeds," an excellent work, which I have found most useful.

I have also received uniform kindness from Professor F. W. Hodge, and Professor W. H. Holmes, of Washington, D. C.; Professor Perkins of Burlington University, Vermont; Warren K. Moorehead, Esq., A. M., of Phillip's Academy (Archaeological Department), Andover, Mass.; C. C. Willoughby, Esq., Peabody Museum, Harvard University; S. S. Rider, Esq.. Providence; the Rev. Joseph Anderson, D.

D., of Waterbury, Conn.; Dr. Benjamin Sharp, of Nantucket; James W. Colby, Esq., of Waltham, Mass.; W. Wallace Tooker, Esq., of Sag Harbor, N. Y. and many other correspondents to whom I now tender grateful acknowledgments.

It is by no means claimed that the lists of Place-names in this volume are exhaustive: I have, however, done my best, and any additional names forwarded to the writer will be gratefully received for future use.

My task has not been an easy one; but if the result is found to supply a want, which I know has been very frequently expressed, in the Public and State Libraries throughout the country, I shall not regret the labor I have expended.

R. A. DOUGLAS-LITHGOW.

BOSTON,
     MASS.

INTRODUCTION

THE AMERICAN–INDIANS IN NEW ENGLAND.

Long previous to the landing of the Pilgrims, at Plymouth, in December, 1620, and for at least a century afterwards, the aborigines, known as Indians, occupied the territory which is now New England, and maintained the same relative positions. It would be manifestly inappropriate here to hazard any opinion as to the original source from which this primitive people emanated, and especially so in the face of the many theories that have already been propounded as to their origin. The whole matter is still a *quæstio vexata*; but, as anthropological research has never, perhaps, been so active and persistent as at present, it is to be hoped that increasing light and knowledge may lead to the elucidation of a problem which has hitherto baffled all efforts for its solution.

The term Indian, as first applied to the American aborigines by early European travellers,— who mistook the American coast for part of Asia,— was an unqualified misnomer: but, when this ancient race was found scattered over the whole land, the same term was used to designate them wherever they were located, and they have been thus uniformly described ever since, although now distinguished as American-Indians, or Amerinds.

MAINE. The aboriginal people identified with Maine consisted of the *Abnaki*, or *Abenaqui*, a confederacy of tribes forming a sub-group of the great Algonquian Stock. The name Abnaki was first applied to the Indians in Nova Scotia, but was afterwards used to designate all the tribes who resided east of Massachusetts, and especially those who inhabited the Western part of Maine, and who frequently overflowed into the northern section of New Hampshire. The name comes from *Wabunaki*, meaning "land or country of the east," or "morning land." It has been recently estimated that they numbered about 2500 in the year 1600. They were divided into the following principal tribes:

The Sokokis or Sochigones, settled on or about the Saco river.

The Arosaguntacooks or Arsikantegou, on or about the Androscoggin river.

The Kanibas, or Norridgewocks, on or about the Kennebec river.

The Penobscots or Pentugouet, on or about the Penobscot river.

The Pequawkets or Pegouakki, in New Hampshire.

The Amaseconti or Aumissoukanti on Farmington Falls, Sandy river.

The Wewenocks or Wawenocks, east of Sagadahoc to St. George's River.

The Rocamekos, a branch of the Pequawkets, at Fryeburg.

The Etchemin tribe inhabited the eastern part of the state, extending from the Penobscot to the St. Croix river, and into New Brunswick as far as St. Johns. Although the earlier writers refer to the Etchemin as a family distinct from the Abnaki, modern anthropologists regard them as descendants of the same original stock, but differing dialectically from them. They are known also as Malecites or Maliseets, and as Passamaquoddies, as in later years, they have resided on the Passamaquoddy river. The Malecites were termed Armouchiquois by the French.

The following additional Abnaki tribes are sometimes referred to but they were so small and unimportant comparatively, as to call for no especial notice. They were the Medoctee, the Muanbessik, the Missiassik, and the Accominta. *Vide* "Tribes."

The various tribes of the Abnaki, while possessing many chiefs or sachems, were alike subject to a supreme ruler, known as the Bashaba, up to 1615, when the last representative of this sovereign office was killed in war. The Wewenocks are said·to have been the immediate subjects of the Great Bashaba. After his death they settled on the west side of the Sheepscot river, near the lower falls. The residence of the Bashaba was in the vicinity of Pemaquid.

MICMACS. Yet another fierce and warlike tribe, known as the Micmacs, must be mentioned as among the northern Indians. These were the aborigines of Acadia or Nova Scotia, and occupied the great peninsula south of the Bay of Fundy: they were also, according to Schoolcraft, the earliest aborigines of the American Continent to come in contact with Europeans. The French designated them as Souriquois, and they had an intense and unvarying hatred of the Etchemin. The term Micmac means "our allies," or "allies." A definition of the smaller tribes will be found among "The American-Indian Tribes of New England," elsewhere in this volume.

NEW HAMPSHIRE. In New Hampshire there were five principal tribes, viz:—Those on the Piscataqua and its branches, to which the name Newichawannocks belonged, although their main residence was on the Cocheco River, near Dover;—the Pequakets, on Saco River,—the Ossipees, on Lake Ossipee, the Coös Indians, the tribes on the Connecticut River, and the various tribes on the Merrimack, and its tributary streams. Of these the Newichawannocks, the Ossipees, the Pequawkets, and the Coös tribes belonged to the Abnaki nation, and the Pequawkets were the most numerous about the time of the arrival of the Pilgrims in 1620. Little is definitely known of the tribes inhabiting the New Hampshire side of the Connecticut River, but they were probably of a mixed character. The Coös Indians who resided in Grafton and Coös Counties are more or less involved in obscurity, but it it surmised that they constituted a comparatively small tribe, and lived for the most part about the junction of the Upper and Lower Ammonoosuc with the Connecticut River, their main dwelling place being situated at the village of Coös or Coosuc, near the mouth of the Lower Ammonoosuc. They were eventually driven off by the English, in 1704, when they joined the St. Francis Indians.

The Nipmuck tribes of New Hampshire, occupying principally the southern section of the state, constituted with the addition of some of the Massachusetts tribes, what is known as the Pennacook confederacy, of which the illustrious Passaconaway was the Bashaba, or ruling chief. The most powerful of all these tribes lived amid the intervales of Pennacook, where the towns of Bow, Concord, and Boscawen are now situated, in Merrimack County. Of the other Confederated tribes the Nashuas occupied the land, on the Nashua River, and the intervales upon the Merrimack. The Souhegans lived upon the Souhegan River and both banks of the Merrimack above and below the mouth of the Souhegan, the Namaoskeags at the Amoskeag Falls, on the Merrimack, in the vicinity of Manchester, and the Winnepesaukees resided in the neighborhood of the lake of that name. The Massachusetts tribes confederated with these consisted mainly of Agawams (Ipswich), the Wamesits or Pawtuckets, (about Lowell), and the Pentuckets (Haverhill). Passaconaway died in 1660.

In 1850 it was stated that "scarcely an Indian remains in the State."

VERMONT. The territory now represented by the State of Vermont was claimed as hunting-ground by the surrounding tribes, and constituted an area frequently traversed by tribes wandering from north to south, or *vice versa*, as well as intersected by numerous shorter routes in varying directions, and this was, if not the main, at least a contributory factor in preventing the aborigines from making Vermont, to any considerable extent, a permanent residence.

Still there are indubitable proofs that the Indians at an early period, must have resided here, and in considerable numbers The St. Francis tribe on the north — (who had their headquarters at Montreal, Hockhelaga as it was then called) — the Narragansets on the the east,—the Pequots on the south,— the Iroquois or Mohawks on the south-west, (Schenectady, Mohawk River, New York)—were the tribes located in the vinicity of Vermont in comparatively recent times. The territory of the Iroquois, eastward, embraced Lake Champlain and the western part of Vermont, and the Indians on the banks of the Susquehanna, Delaware, Hudson and Connecticut Rivers were in a kind of subjection to them.*

History records the scantiest information concerning the Indians in Vermont, and the Amerind Place and Proper names throughout the Green-Mountain State are so few as to but em-

---

* Dr. S. Williams, *History of Vermont*, 1809.

phasize the fact that the only remaining traces of her aborigines
have almost faded away for ever.

MASSACHUSETTS. Of the *Massachusetts* tribes that bearing
the name of this State had dominion, for the most part, over the
eastern territory adjacent to Massachusetts Bay: there is,
however, little positive evidence forthcoming as to either the
limitations of their territory or their power, as, some time about
1617, the tribe was decimated by a pestilence and thoroughly
disorganized by warfare. Soon after this period their territory
seems to have been divided amongst the Nipmucks, Narragansets
and other tribes. That they formerly sustained a position of importance in the state is evidenced by Gookin who says that their
chief sachem held dominion over many petty governors, as, for
example, those of Weymouth, Neponsit and Punkapoag, and that
his suzerainty extended to Newton Nashaway etc., and as far
as Deerfield, into the heart of the Nipmuck country. Moreover,
Johnson seems to have regarded them more as a confederacy
than as a tribe, and described the group as formerly having
"three kingdoms or sagamoreships, having under them seven
dukedoms or petty sagamores." It also appears that they were
either tributary to, or in alliance with the Narragansets.

According to Hubbard, the mouth of the Charles River was
a rendezvous of all the Indians north and south, and Hutchinson says that the "circle which now makes the harbours of
Boston and Charlestown, round by Malden, Chelsea, Nantasket,
Hingham, Braintree, Weymouth, and Dorchester, was the
Capital of a great sachem;" and the tradition is that he had his
principal seat on a hill * near Dorchester, in the neighborhood
of Squantum. Whether this was the great sachemdom of the
Massachusetts Indians or not cannot now be absolutely stated,
but it may be inferred as very probable. Chickataubit and
Wampatuck, his son, were sachems of this tribe, and the names
of at least eight other sachems are known. The sachemdom of
Chickataubit was at Weymouth. He was probably subject to
the Wampanoags, and his principal residence was at Tehticut,
near Namasket, now Middleborough.

---

* Messatsoosec Hill.

This tribe, it is stated, at one time aggregated 3000 warrior but it is more likely that this number was in excess of all the members of the tribe. Chickataubit died of small-pox about 1633.

NIPMUCKS. The Nipmuck tribe dwelt, for the most part, in the eastern interior of Massachusets, and occupied many of the lakes and rivers, especially in Worcester and the adjacent counties. Although the actual limitation of their territory is now indeterminate, it must have been very extensive, as it appears from a XVIIth century map that their boundaries formerly reached as far as Boston, on the east,—as far south as the divisional line of Connecticut and Rhode Island,*— westward as far as Bennington, in Vermont, and in a northern direction at least as far as Concord, New Hampshire, as we have already seen. We are at least assured that they dominated the banks of the Merrimack from Lowell, Mass., to Concord, N. H. One of the favorite seats of the sachems of this tribe was said to have been at Wachusett mountain, near Princeton, in the northern part of Worcester County. Another centre was probably near Medford, Mystic Pond, where their great, and probably last sachem, Nanepashemet, lived, and where he was killed, in 1619.†

In addition to the many Indian centres throughout the interior, Nipmuck Sachemdoms also existed at Saugus, (Lynn) at Nahant, Nahumkeag, (Salem), Marblehead, and round the Essex coast. It is, however, probable that many of these originally belonged to the Massachusetts Indians, and that they were transferred to the Nipmucks after the disorganisation of the Massachusetts tribe.

Of the several tribes which inhabited the shores of Massachusetts and Plymouth Bays, the most important was, perhaps, that known as the WAMPANOAGS or POKANOKETS who were considered as the third greatest nation in New England when it was settled by the English, and when "the good Massassoit" was their chief sachem or king. It has been asserted that his sovereignty

---

* They also "occupied a territory covering the northern portion of Rhode Island." Sidney S. Rider.

† Shattuck's *History of Concord.*

included all the territory "from Cape Cod and all that part of Massachusetts and of Rhode Island between Narraganset and Massachusetts Bays and inward between Pawtucket and Charles River." Whatever doubt there may be about these limitations, it must be conceded that the Wampanoags exercised some sway over at least, the petty tribes of the interior, while their own territory extended from Massachusetts Bay to Cape Cod, and through the disputed tracts north of the Narraganset country to the bay bearing the same name.* In this connection it is a curious fact that King Philip, son of Massassoit, and one of his successors, could not induce the Nauset Indians of Cape Cod to take part in his disastrous war of 1675-6.

The principal residence of the great chiefs of the Wampanoags was called Pokanoket, or Mount Hope, now included in Bristol, R. I.

RHODE ISLAND. The *Narraganset* territory was stated † to extend to Pawtucket River, Brookfield, and the Blackstone River, in a northerly direction, westerly to Wickabaug Pond, at West Brookfield, southerly to the ocean and on the east by Narraganset Bay: or as Gookin says‡ about 30 or 40 miles from Sekunk River and Narraganset Bay, including Rhode Island and the other islands in that Bay. Roughly speaking, therefore, their boundaries are represented by the State of Rhode Island as it is to-day.

During the first half of the 17ᵗʰ century the rule of this belligerent and formidable tribe was effectively administered by their two great sachems Canonicus and Miantunnomoh, and, in 1642, they were, perhaps, the strongest, as well as the most warlike of the New England Indians. Although the estimates of their numbers vary very considerably, it is fair to assume that, at this time, the tribe aggregated between 4 and 5000. Their warfare with the Wampanoags, the Pequots, the Mohegans and the English gradually reduced their strength, and the steady advance of the white settlers within the confines of New Eng-

---

*G. L. Austin, *History of Mass.*
† Mass. H. S. Col., 3, 1, 210.
‡ *History of Praying Indians.*

land had so diminished them that, in a little over a century, this great nation was reduced to only a few hundred persons.

The *Nehantics* or *Niantics* constituted a branch of the Narragansetts, and their greatest sachem was Ninigret: the principal residence of the tribe was at Wickabaug, now Westerly, R. I. A section of this tribe resided in Connecticut, when they were known as the Western Niantics.

CONNECTICUT. The Pequots were if not the most numerous, the most formidable as well as the fiercest and bravest of the aborigines of Connecticut. They, together with the Mohegans, belonged originally to the same race as the Mahicans, Mohicanders, or Machanders who resided on the banks of the Hudson. The territory they claimed as their own represented an area of about five hundred square miles, and it extended from the Niantic River, on the west, to Wecapaug, ten miles east of the Pawcatuck River, which divides Connecticut from Rhode Island;— their most northern clans, the Mohegans, extending northward for a distance of about 10 or 12 miles from Long Island Sound: in fine, the suzerainty of their chief sachem was, at one time, said to extend from Narraganset to Hudson River, and all along the Connecticut shore, including Long Island.

Although their numbers have been estimated as aggregating 4000, the probability is that the tribe never exceeded 2000; but almost incessant warfare, and especially the war against the combined Narragansets, Mohegans, and the English, in 1638, completed their overthrow, and they ultimately became the subjects of the white settlers. In 1680, the estimate of the General Court as to the number of the Indians in Connecticut amounted to only 500 warriors as representing about 2500 individuals.

Throughout the State of Connecticut, there were many Indian tribes of comparatively minor importance, such as the Paugussets and Wepawaugs, the Potatucks, the Quinnipiacs, the Hammonassets, and the Tunxis, also the so-called River tribes living on the banks of the Connecticut River, consisting of the Podunks, and the Wangunks: none of these, however, calls for detailed attention here.*

---

* The respective locations of these tribes will be found in "The Principal American-Indian tribes of New England" elsewhere in this work.

Sassacus was the chief Sachem of the Pequots, and a man who terrorised all the neighboring tribes. He was said to have had 26 sachems under him, and his principal residence was on the River Thames, near New London.

The MOHEGANS. Uncas, Pequot sachem of Mohegan, was a direct descendant of the royal line of the tribe. He married the daughter of Sassacus the Chief Sachem, in 1626, thus strengthening his claims to the tribal sachemdom, and subsequently rebelled against his father-in-law (1634-5?) and was defeated and banished. In 1638 he entered into a treaty with the English in Connecticut, and the Narragansets, and his following, growing in numbers and importance, he was gradually raised to a position of considerable influence and independent power. Uncas died in 1682 or 3. In the history of his race he was probably never excelled in personal bravery, or as a diplomatic strategist.

The territory of the Mohegans, although its limitations have not been very clearly defined, may be said, roughly, to have extended from a short distance from the Connecticut River, on the south "to a space of disputed country on the north, next the Narragansets." The number of the Mohegans cannot well be estimated with any degree of accuracy. Dr. Williamson in his *History of Maine* computes it as 3000, but as this estimate is made as representing the year 1615, and therefore long before the division of the Pequots took place, it cannot be accepted as either accurate or reliable. My own impression is that the Mohegans were never very numerous—probably under 2000—but that the skilful diplomacy of Uncas enabled them to take a foremost place in the history of the period during which they flourished.

PRAYING INDIANS.

A few words may be devoted to the consideration of the Natick or Praying Indians, a sect developed among the Massachusetts tribe and other converts, in 1646, owing principally to the missionary efforts of Rev. John Eliot, who so far mastered the difficulties of the local Indian dialect as enabled him to translate the Bible into it. From 1646 to 1674 the joint efforts of Messrs. Eliot, Gookin, Mayhew, and others resulted in founding a small school of "Christian Indians" in the following places:—Punkapoag (Stoughton); Hassanamessit (Grafton); Okommakamesit (Marlborough); Wamesit (Tewksbury) Nash-obah (Littleton); Magunkaquog (Hopkinton); Manchauge (Oxford); Chabanakongkomun, (Dudley); Maanexit, (Wood-stock); Wabquissit (also in Woodstock); Pachachoog (partly in Worcester); Weshakim (Nashaway); Waentug, (Uxbridge); and Natick. In 1674 the missionaries claimed to have con-verted about 1150 persons, being the aggregate of their converts in all these fourteen towns; but, after 1675 (when Philip's war was in progress), the believers dwindled down to about 300, and, six years after the war, Mr. Eliot could only claim four towns. I am merely stating facts, and make no comment further than to quote the following from Dr Douglass' *Summary* *: — "Mr Eliot," he says, "with immense labor translated and printed our Bible into Indian. It was done with a good, pious design, but it must be reckoned among the *otiosorum hominum negotia:* [the achievements of leisurely men]: it was done in the Natick (Mass.) language. Of the Naticks at present (1745) there are not 20 families subsisting, and scarce any can read. *Cui boni?*"

The foregoing outline of the Amerind tribes of New England will, it is hoped, sufficiently indicate the respective locations of the aboriginal inhabitants. With regard to their aggregate tribal numbers many opinions have been expressed and many estimates given by some of the earlier writers, but most of them have been as rash as extravagant. More careful recent inquiry has elicited the fact that the number of Indians occupying New England, at any time subsequent to the year 1600, has been very much exaggerated, and the writer has been assured by two well-known modern anthropologists, who have made a special study of the matter, that the total number of Indians in New England about the year 1600 did not exceed 24, or 25,000. Their calculations, arrived at independently, are based upon an

---

* Vol. 1, p. 172, *note*.

average of between 75 to 80 souls in each village, and the results are as follows:—

Pequots,	2000
Narragansetts,	5000
Massachusetts,	2500
Wampanoags,	3000
Pawtuckets,	2000
Mohegans,	2000
Maine Indians,	2500
All others,	2500
Total,	21,500

The aboriginal inhabitants of the American Continent were foredoomed from the time that European travellers discovered its natural wealth and attractiveness, and began to make settlements upon its productive shores: and when, in 1620, the Pilgrims landed in Plymouth Bay, they brought with them the seeds of a more advanced civilisation which, when cultivated among them, took deep root in the soil, and spread their benignant growths in every direction.

The poor Indians had little chance against such a development, and although, in their primitive and inchoate condition, they were unfitted to withstand the gradually increasing inroads of a more resourceful race, yet the history of their conquests records deeds of bravery,—of self-sacrifice, and of exalted patriotism which no nation has ever excelled.

An opinion, too generally shared, which regards the American-Indian race as mere savages, almost inhuman in their ferocity and cruelty, and without a redeeming feature of any kind, is as untrue as it is unjust. They naturally possessed those characteristics shared by all unenlightened races of men who have been deprived of the elevating influence of civilization, and a high code of ethics, but a careful study of their lives and history shows that, according to their enlightenment, they were actuated by many virtues which, in superior races, count for dignified manhood and nobility of mind. In personal bravery and courage they had few equals, and yet they accepted conquest or punishment with a sublime fortitude and stoicism which scorned to ask for either life or pardon. Equality, freedom and independence constituted the very atmosphere of their being, and in their dealings with their own race the right of each individual and his personal freedom and liberty were universally acknowledged. Judged from our modern standard the principles of morality which governed their lives, if of a lower order, were yet in keeping with their instincts and their environment, and they believed that the crimes of the vicious were punished by the disgrace, contempt, and danger they ensured for transgressors.

In their domestic relationships they were generally faithful and commendable; marital unfaithfulness was regarded as a crime, and Roger Williams gives instances in which married Indians had resided together in mutual trust and quietude for 20, 30, 40, and even 50 years. They treated their children with affection and indulgence, choosing rather to mould their characters by means of reason and persuasion than to use harsher measures.

Robbery, and murder for the sake of robbery, were extremely rare amongst them, and, if they had little idea of the beauty and value of truth, it was because they knew no better. They were loyal to their chiefs and their people, prudent and wise in council, sagacious and intelligent,—extremely hospitable both to strangers and friends, grateful for all benefits received, and ever generous toward each other when fortune seemed to befriend them.

That they were resentful of injury, and revengeful towards their enemies must be admitted, but the conduct of the white settlers towards them was in nowise calculated to repress the activities of Nature's first and dominating law of self-preservation. The history of their gradual extermination forms the darkest pages in the history of their successors, and it was fortunate that the pioneers of New England secured, through the broad-mindedness and generosity of good old Massassoit, the friendliness of the Wampanoags, or another and a different story might have had to be told.

When all that can be said against the Indians has been spoken it must be conceded that they embodied a pure and lofty patriotism for which they fought and died like men and true patriots, and although they had to gradually yield up their possessions and their homes in the land they loved, and to recede and disappear before the advancing wave of civilisation, yet as De Forest says; "We may drop a tear over the grave of the race which has perished, and regret that civilisation and christianity have ever accomplished so little for its amelioration."

ABBREVIATED REFERENCES

H. H. Mass.	Hutchinson's History of Massachusetts Bay.
Mass. Bay Col. Rec.	Massachusetts-Bay Colonial Records.
Mass. H. S. Col.	Massachusetts Historical Society's Collections.
N. H. H. S. Col.	New Hampshire Historical Society's Collections.
R. I. H. S. Col.	Rhode Island Historical Society's Collections.
M. H. S. Col.	Maine Historical Society's Collections.
Conn. H. S. Col.	Connecticut Historical Society's Collections.
Plym. Rec.	Plymouth Colonial Records.
Plym. Rec. Judl.	Plymouth Judicial Records.
Col. Rec.	Colonial Records of Connecticut.
Col. Rec. Lands.	Records of Lands etc., Secretary's Office, Hartford, Conn.
New. Y. Col.	New York Collections.
Hampden Co. Records.	"Indian Deeds." H. A. Wright.
H.-B. of A.-I.	Hand-Book of American Indians: Bureau of Ethnology.
Rider's Map.	Preceding "Lands of Rhode Island," by S. S. Rider.
Smith.	Captain John Smith, Navigator, 1614.
R. W.	Roger Williams.
J. H. T.	Dr. J. Hammond Trumbull.
S. G. D.	Samuel G. Drake.
G.	Moses Greenleaf.
J. G. C.	Hon. J. G. Crawford.
S. G. B.	Stanley G. Boyd, "Indian Local Names."
L. L. H.	Lucius L. Hubbard. "Woods and Lakes of Maine."
Suffolk Rec. or Suff. Rec.	"Suffolk Deeds." Vol. I to XIII.
Church's History.	"Church's Indian Wars, 1675—1704:" edited by S. G. Drake.
De Forest.	"History of the Indians of Conn.," by J. W. DeForest. 1851.
Moh.	Mohegan.
Nip.	Nipmuck.
Narr.	Narraganset.
Quinnip.	Quinnipiac.
Quineb.	Quinebaug.
Peq.	Pequot.

NATIVE AMERICAN
PLACE NAMES
OF
MASSACHUSETTS

MASSACHUSETTS

Aberjona River, at Winchester.

Abouset River, near Charles River.   H. H. Mass. Vol. 1, p. 15.
Abbouset River, near Charles River.

Abbaquackea tract, southwest of Groton, beyond Nashaway River (1668).   Mass. Bay Col. Rec. Vol. IV, Part 2, p. 384.

Acashewah, occurs in Philip's deed, 1671.   *Vide* Acushena.

Acawmuck, near Plymouth. "To go by water?" Mass. H. S. Col. 2d, Vol. 3.

Acchushnutt River, New Bedford.   Mass. H. S. Col. 1st, X, 129–134 (1809).

Accomac, early name of Plymouth; "land on the other side, or beyond the water."

Accomonticus, Boston; "beyond the hill-little-cove."   Ogilby, 1671.   *Vide* Abnaki synonym,—Agamenticus, Me.

Accoomeck, Plymouth, *Vide* Acawmuck. Governor Winthrop. Mass. H. S. Col. 2d, Vol. 3.

Accoomeneck.
Acoomemeck, "of which Massassoit was sachem."   Winthrop, 1638.

Acoont River, "Sepaconit," near Marion, Plymouth Co.

Acoakset, Westport, Bristol Co.
Acoakset River, Westport, Bristol Co.

Acockus tract.

Aconnquesse, west side of Point Peril.

Acoughcouss.

Acquiatt neck, Yarmouth. *Vide* Alquiod. Plym. Rec. Vol. 2, p. 21.

Acqussent River, "which flows into Neckatay." Plym. Rec. Vol. 2, p. 11.

Acushena, early name of Dartmouth territory.

Acushnet Village, site of New Bedford.

Acushnet River, New Bedford.

Agawam, Ipswich, "a fishing station,"—"fish-curing place," or "ground overflowed by water."

Agawam, Springfield. "Resort for the fish of passage,"—"ground overflowed by water."

Agawam, at Westfield River, near Springfield. "Ground over-flowed by water."

Agawam, Wareham, Plymouth Co. "Fish-curing" (place). "Lowland," "marsh" or "meadow."

Agawam River, Wareham, Plymouth Co.

Agowaywam, part of Wareham: same as Agawam. 1622.

Ahampatunshauge Pond, Worcester Co.

Ahumpatunshauge Pond, Worcester Co.

Ahquannissowamsoo River, north side of Teticut River (Cotuh-tikut).

Ahquaunauwansuh. Plym. Rec. Vol. 2, 238 (Judicial).

Ahquonsooawmsooh. Plym. Rec. Vol. 1, 232.

Ahquonsoonumsoo. Plym. Rec. Vol. 1, 232.

Akusenag, Dartmouth. *Vide* Acushena.

Alum Pond, Sturbridge, Worcester Co. (source of Quinebaug River), probably derived from Allumps, sachem of Quinebaug, or from Indian word signifying "a dog." *Vide* Allum, Conn.

Alum Pond, Little, Holland, Worcester Co.

Amaganset? *Vide* "Indian Names of Boston," Horsford, 1886.

Anaquakett, same as Nanaquakett, q. v.

Anequeasset tract, near Rochester. "Striped squirrels."

Anequeassett tract, near Rochester. "Striped squirrels."

Anmoughcawgen, early name of Newton and Cambridge territory. *Vide* Aumoughcawgen.

Annasnappet River, East Middleton.

Annawamcoate, Plymouth Co.

Annawon Rock, Rehoboth. Name derived from that of Annawan, one of Philip's distinguished warriors.

Annisnippi Brook, near Scituate. "Rocky water." *Vide* Assinippi.

Annisquam, near Gloucester. "At the top, or point, of the rock."

Annisquam Harbour, near Gloucester.

Annursuack Hill, near Concord.

Annursuc Hill, near Concord.

Annussanatonsett River, Pocasset. Plym. Rec. Vol. 1, p. 239.

Anquepinick, near Sunderland, Franklin; "the inclined land." H. A. Wright.

Apaum, early Indian name of Plymouth.

Aponaganset, Dartmouth. *Vide* Potagansett, Conn. and Ponaganset, R. I.

Aponecett tract, near Rochester.

Apponagansett River. *Vide* Aponaganset.

Apponagansett Harbour.

Aquaquesett meadows, near Mattakeeset. Plym. Rec. Vol. 3, p. 144.

Aquausowonso River, flowing into Teticut River. Plym. Rec. Vol. 1, pp. 232–3 (1695).
Aquausowouso. *Vide* Ahquannissowamsoo.

Aquetnet, Sandwich, Barnstable Co., "at an island." Mass. H. S. Col. 2d, Vol. IV, p. 293.

Aquidnose tract, Nantucket, 1687.

Aquitnet Point, Nantucket Deed, 1722.

Aquonest Pond, near Satucket. Plym. Rec. Vol. 5, p. 109 (1672–3).

Aqunoonogqutut tract, Nantucket Deed. Jan. 9th, 1668.

Asabeth River. *Vide* Assabeth and Assabet.

Ascopompamocke, near Rochester.

Ascoochames tract, near Rochester.

Ashimuit Village, at junction of Mashpee, Falmouth and Sandwich. 1674. *Vide* Ashumet.

Ashquoach, Brimfield, Worcester Co., "the ending place."
Ashquoach Hill, West Brookfield, Worcester Co.
Ashquoash, West Brookfield. Mass. H. S. Col. Vol. 1 (1806).

Ashuelot, Dalton, Berkshire.
Ashuelot, Swansea, Bristol Co.

Ashumet Pond, Mashpee. "A spring," same as Ashimuit, q. v.
Ashunet Pond, Mashpee. "A spring."

Asnacancomic Pond, Hubbardston, "a long house of stones." *Vide* Asnacomet.
Asnacomet Pond, Hubbardston.

Asnebumsket Hill, Paxton, Worcester Co. "where a standing rock is on a stony foundation."

Asneconcomet Pond, Hubbardston. "Long stone house," or "house of stones."

Asneconic Pond, Hubbardston. *Vide* Asnacomet.

Asnemscutt Pond, near Namasket River.

Asneoumsket Pond, near Paxton, Worcester Co.

Asnuntuck River, Longmeadow. "Stony River."

Aspomsok Hill, Holden, Worcester Co., supposed to be a corruption of Asnebumsket. Washburn.

Aspowunck, Easthampton, Hampden Co. "A place where nets are set." Hamp. Co. Rec. Wright.

Aspowounk.

Asquenunseck, West Springfield.

Assabasset. "A drinking-place where the water is broad."

Assabet, Northborough. "It is miry." *Indian Bulletin,* 1867.

Assabet Village, Maynard, Middlesex.

Assabet River, Berlin. Possibly "at the drinking place."

Assabet Mount, Northborough.

Assabeth River. *Vide* Asabeth and Assabet.

Assameekq tract, near Dartmouth. Bristol Co. H-B. A-I. p. 102, Vol. 1.

Assanippi Brook, near Scituate. "Rocky water." *Vide* Assinippi.

Assattayyagg, Easthampton. Hamp. Co. Rec. "Poplar-tree land." H. A. Wright.

Assawanupsit, Lakeville, Plymouth Co. *Vide* Assawompsett. Mass. H. S. Col.

Assawomit, part of Middleborough. *Vide* Assoowamsoo.

Assawompsett, Lakeville, Plymouth Co.

Assawompsett Pond, Lakeville, Plymouth Co.

Assowamsit Neck, Lakeville, Plymouth Co.

Assinippi settlement, Hanover.

Assinippi Brook, Hanover. "Rocky water."

Assonet Village, Freetown, Bristol.

Assonet Bay, Freetown, Bristol.

Assonet Neck, Freetown, Bristol.

Assonet River, Freetown, Bristol.

The ancient inhabitants of Assonet were supposed to be the authors of the "Dighton Rock" inscriptions.

As soowamsoo, part of Middleborough; same as Assawomit, q. v.

Atquiod Neck, Yarmouth. Plym. Rec. Vol. 2, p. 21.

Astimmoost, Nantucket. Deed, June 5th, 1677.

Attaquahunchonitt Neck, Mashpee; east side of Wequaket River. Plym. Rec. Vol. VI, p. 160.

Attitash Lake, near Amesbury;—"a huckleberry."

Aucoot Cove, near Mattapoiset.

Auguan, early form of Agawam. Smith, 1631.

Augutteback Pond, Oxford. Possibly "Kettle Pond."

Auhquannissonwaumissoo River, Teticut River. *Vide* Ahquannissowamsoo.

Aumoughcawgen. *Vide* Anmoughcawgen.

Auntaanta meadow, near Mashpee.

Ausotunoog. *Vide* Housatonic.

Autopscot, Nantucket. Dr. B. Sharp.

B

Babbitasset, a former village in Pepperell, now included in East Pepperell. Dr. S. A. Green.

Baddacook, a pond in eastern part of old Groton. Dr. S. A. Green.

Baquaug River, same as Payquage, now Miller's River. *Vide* Mrs. Rowlandson's "Narrative," p. 64.

Bashapish Falls, Mount Washington, Berkshire.

Bashbish Mountain, Mt. Washington range. Said to have been named from an Indian squaw called"Bess."

Bashbish Stream, Taconic mountains, Berkshire.

Bellyhac Hill? Great Swamp, Salem.

Bermaken.

Big Mystic Pond, Winchester.

Bimilick Brook, Worcester; named from Indian sachem.

Boggestow Brook, Medway, Norfolk.

Boggestow, Sherborn, Middlesex.

Boggochoag Hills, Worcester. Mass. H. S. Col. Vol. 1, p. 113. *Vide* Packachoag.

Buddacook Pond, near Groton.

C

Canesto Brook, Hubbardston.

Cannestow River, Barre, Worcester Co.

Canopache, east end of Nantucket, "a place of peace."

Canoza Lake, near Amesbury.

Capaum Pond, Nantucket.

Capawack, Martha's Vineyard. Winthrop.
Capawock.

Capawong Brook, Whately, Franklin Co.

Capawonk meadow, west side of Connecticut River, Hampden Co.

Cape Poge Pond, Edgartown, Dukes Co.

Capoge, Martha's Vineyard.

Capowonk meadow, now in Hatfield. Judd's *History of Hadley*. "where the stream is shut in." H. A. Wright. *Vide* Matta-omet.

Cappowongamick, west of Kuppawonkunchk. "Place shut in by a bend." J. H. T. *Vide* Kuppawonkunchk.

Cappowong. *Vide* Capawonk.

Caskakachesquash tract, near Assawompsett. Plym. Rec. Vol. 1, p. 229.

Cataconamog Pond, Lunenburg, Worcester Co.

Catacoonamug Pond, Lunenburg. "Great long fishing-place."

Catacunnemug Brook, Shirley, Middlesex. "Great long fishing-place."

Catcheckawitt Pond, Andover. *Vide* Cochitewick.

Catecunemaug Pond, Lunenburg. *Vide* Catacoonamug.

Cateconimoug Pond, Lunenburg.

Cattacapcheise field, Plymouth. Plym. Rec.   1, p. 27.

Cautaugcanteest.

Cautaugeanteest Hill, south of Plymouth. *Vide* Cautaugcanteest. Plym. Rec. Vol. 1, p. 41.

Cataumet Harbour, Falmouth.

Cataumet Village, Falmouth.

Cataumet Neck, Falmouth.

Cattones Akees, Hatfield. A corruption of Cottinackeesh, q. v. H. A. Wright.

Cawsumsett Neck, near Patucket River. Plym. Rec. Vol. 3, p. 167. (1679.)

Chabanakongkomun, land near Dudley. *Vide* Chaubunakonga-muk. (Gookin.)

Chaboken Pond, Harvard. "Hell Pond."

Chachaubunkakowok. Nipmuck village. A-I. H-B. Vol. 11.

Chanagongum, contraction for Chaubunakongkomuk. "Boundary fishing-place."

Chapnocunco Pond? Suff. Rec. 344, Vol. XIII, 1684.

Chapnocunco tract? "land of Tacomus." Suff. Rec. 344, Vol. XIII, 1684.

Chappapemeset, Nantucket. Deed. July 1st, 1690.

Chappaquiddick, Edgartown, Dukes. "Separated island."

Chappaquiddick Island, Edgartown, Dukes. "Separated island."

Chappaquonset Creek, Martha's Vineyard.

Chappaquonset, Tisbury, Dukes.

Chappaquonsit Pond, Tisbury, Dukes.

Chappaquoit Island, West Falmouth. *Vide* Chassaquoit.

Chappaquoit Point, West Falmouth.

Chargoggagogmanchogagog, Webster. *Vide* Chaubunagungamaug. "Fishing-place at the boundary." Freeland.

Chassaquoit Point, West Falmouth.

Chaubaqueduck, at Martha's Vineyard. "Separated island." *Vide* Chappaquiddick.

Chaubunakongamuk, name of land about Webster. "Boundary fishing-place."

Chaubunagungamaug, same as preceding.

Chebacco, Essex.

Chebacco Lake, Hamilton, Essex.

Checkaby River. *Vide* Chicopee. Mass. Bay Col. Rec. 4, part 2, p. 436.

Cheekwakat, a name for Barnstable.

Chepachewest, Sandwich. *Vide* Pacheweset.

Chequapee, Hampden Co. "Cedar land," or "Birch-bark place." *Vide* Chicopee.

Chequesset, Wellfleet.

Chequocket, Provincetown.

Chesquonapoage Pond, Lancaster. "The great long pond."
Chesquonopog Pond.

Chessawanacke Island, near Mt. Hope Neck. Plym. Rec. Vol. 2, p. 256. (Judicial.)

Chicabee.
Chicopee Mountain, Springfield, Hampden Co.
Chicopee River, "violent water."
Chicopee Falls.
Chickopee City, near Springfield.
Chickopee Co.

Chickataubut Hill, Milton. Name derived from that of sachem.

Chickons, Indian Hollow, Hatfield, Hampden Co., "a little kettle;" "a hollow." H. A. Wright.

Chippascuit, a tract south of Mastucksett River, Taunton.
Chippascutt. Plym. Rec. Vol. 1, p. 242.

Chippaquiddick, Edgartown, Dukes. "Separated island."
Chippoquiddick. *Vide* Chappaquiddick.

Chissawonook Island, near Mt. Hope Neck, Hog Island. Plym. Rec. Vol. 2, p. 276.
Chisawamicke. *Vide* Chessawanacke. Plym. Rec. Vol. 2, p. 250.

Chobocco. *Vide* Chebacco and Tchobocco. W. Wood. 1634.
Chocame tract, Tisbury and Chilmark. M. H. S. Col. 2, 2d, 378.

Chockolog Pond, Uxbridge. Name probably transferred from land.

Chocksett, Sterling, Worcester Co.

Chocksett land, near Sterling, Worcester Co. *Vide* Woonsechocksett.

Chupipoggut Pond, bounding Nahleawamet Neck, Middleborough. Plym. Rec. Vol. 1, p. 235.

Chuppateest, Coney Island or Neck, Manomet Bay.

Chusick Brook, South Hadley, Hampden Co. Rec. A. 8. Wright.

Coakset, Dartmouth.

Coasatke, part of tract at Wasqakage, q. v. Indian deed, 1671. Probably "Pine-tree place."

Coasuck Brook, Mill Brook, Northfield. "Pine-tree place." Wright.

Coassit, "56 miles above Hadley," Worcester Co. "At the pines." Appleton, 1675. An Indian rendezvous.

Coosuc Village, mouth of Lower Ammonoosuc. H-B. of A-I., p. 342. *Vide* N. H. The former of these two names is supposed to be identical with the latter. *Ibid*, 316.

Coatue, a neck of land at Nantucket.

Coatuit, Osterville, Barnstable (1674), a praying village.

Coatuit, a name also applied to Provincetown.

Coaxet, Dartmouth. *Vide* Coakset, applied also to a village near Little Compton, R. I.

Cocasset Pond, Foxborough.

Cochao Brook, Randolph.

Cochato River, Braintree.

Cocheset Village, near West Bridgewater, Plymouth Co. *Vide* Coweset. "Place of small pine-trees."

Cochessett, Brockton.

Cochichawick, Andover. "Place of the great cascade."   N. H. H. Col. Vol. VIII, 451.

Cochichawick Lake, North Andover.   "At the wild dashing stream."

Cochichawick River, North Andover.   "At the wild dashing stream."

Cochichowick.   Mass. Bay Col. Rec. Vol. 1, 257.

Cochichawicke, Andover.   *Vide supra.*

Cochickowicke, Andover.   *Vide* Cochichawick.

Cochitawake, Andover.

Coijchawick, Andover.

Coojetawick, Andover.   *Vide* Quichechacke, Quyachick, etc.

Cochituate Village, Middlesex Co.   "Land on rapid streams."

Cochituate Lake, Natick.   "Very deep water?"   *Indian Bulletin,* 1867.

Cocyeania Valley, Nantucket.   Deed, 1687.

Codtanmeet, in Mashpee.   Gookin.

Coddude, Nantucket.   Deed, 1690.   *Vide* Coatue?

Cohann, Neponset.   R. I. H. S. Col. Vol. IV.

Cohanit, Raynham, Bristol Co., "a long place"?

Cohannet, Taunton, Bristol Co., "a long place"?

Cohasset Brook, Southbridge: "a fishing promontory."

Cohasse, Southbridge, Worcester Co., "a fishing promontory." *Vide* Cohasset.

Cohasset, Norfolk Co.   *Vide* Connohasset.

Cohasset Harbour, Norfolk Co.

Coicus, same as Nonacoicus, Ayer and Groton, q. v.   Dr. S. A. Green.

Comassakumkanit, a settlement at Herring Pond, Plymouth, Bourne.

Comessett tract, near Hingham.   Suff. Rec. 244, Vol. 1.

Commet.   *Vide* Asnacancomic.
Comet.

Conconut Hollow, near Great Swamp, Salem.

Conesto Brook, Hubbardston, Worcester Co.

Congamond, Southwick, Hampden.
Congamond Ponds, Southwick, Hampden.

Congamuck Pond.   *Vide* Congamond.

Conihast.   Suff. Rec. 244, Vol. 1.

Conihosset.   *Vide* Cohasset and Connohasset.   *New England's Prospect.*   Wood.   1634.

Connohasset, same as Cohasset, q. v.   "Fishing Promontory," 1635.

Conomo Point, West Gloucester.

Coonemesset Pond, Hatchville, Barnstable.
Coonemosset Pond, Hatchville, Barnstable.

Cooxit, Dartmouth.   *Vide* Coakset.   H. H. Mass. 1, 313.

Cooxissett Village, Plymouth Co.   Mass. H. S. Col. 4th, Vol. V, p. 143.   (Hinckley.)

Copecut Hill, Fall River, Bristol Co.
Copecut River, Freetown, Bristol Co.

Coppoanissett, same as Penguine Hole, q. v.   Plym. Rec. Vol, 1, p. 239

Coquitt, Dartmouth.   Gookin.

Coskata Pond, Nantucket.

Coskata Beach, Nantucket.

Coskaty, part of Nantucket, same as Koskata, q. v.

Cotochta, Nantucket. Dr. B. Sharp.

Cottinackeesh, near Agawam, Springfield. "Plantation-ground."

Cottinyakies, Hampden Co. Rec. Wright.

Cottochusett, Osterville, Barnstable.

Cottoyowsekeesett, near Rochester.

Cottochesett Neck, Barnstable Co.

Cotochesett Neck. *Vide* Cottochusett and Cottoyowsekeesett.

Cotuhtikut River, same as Teticut, q. v.

Cotuhicut River, same as Teticut, q. v.

Coteticut River, same as Teticut, q. v. M. H. S. Col. 7, 2d, 291.

Cotuit. *Vide* Coatuit. 1674.

Cotuit River, Osterville or Mashpee, Barnstable.

Cotukticut land, part of Middleborough.

Coutoocook River, Haverhill. "Crow-river."

Cowachuck, South Hadley, Hampden Co. Rec. A. 8. *Vide* Quaquoonuntuck and Cowase.

Cowas. *Vide* Coasuck.

Cowase Brook, South Hadley. Hampden Co. Rec. A. 8. H. A. Wright.

Cowasset River, said to be the same as Sippiqunnet, q. v. "Place of pines."

Cowassock Brook, near Framingham.

Cowate Village, Charles River, Middlesex Co. 1677. Gookin.

Cowate Falls, Charles River, Middlesex Co. Gookin.

Coweset land, Wareham.

Coweset Village, near West Bridgewater, Plymouth Co. *Vide* Cocheset.

Cowsett Brook, North Bridgewater, Plymouth Co.

Coxit, same as Coquitt and Coakset, q. v. Gookin.

Coychawicke, Mass. Bay Col. Rec. Vol. 1, 257. *Vide* Cochichowick.

Cromeset Point, Wareham, Plymouth Co.

Cummaquid, Barnstable.

Cummaquid Harbour, Barnstable.

Cushnet, New Bedford. *Vide* Acushnet.

Cuttyhunk, Dukes Co., a contraction of a word meaning "a thing that lies out in the water."

Cuttyhunk Island, Dukes Co.

Cuttyhunk Harbour, Dukes Co.

D

Deowcook, Rattlesnake Peak, Taconic Range. "Hill of the wolves."

E

Equies Brook. Probably a corruption of the name of a Mohegan sachem,—Tantoquieson. *Vide* "Proper Names."

Equies Swamp.

F

Fennapoo? or Bowditch's Ledge, Baker's Island.

G

Gassetk, near Hadley, Hampden Co. "The little wood," or "a place where the wood is small." H. A. Wright.

Gesquoquaset, a tract near Nauset (Eastham).

Gotomska, Westport.

Gushee Pond, North Raynham, Plymouth Co.

H

Haquesukkuppamuke tract, Pocasset. Plym. Rec. Vol. 1, p. 241.

Harcomonco Pond, Worcester Co.

Hashkinnit-chaopket tract, Nantucket. Deed, Jan. 9th, 1668.

Hasnebumskitt Hill, near Holden. *Vide* Asnebumskit.
Hasnebumskeat Hill, near Holden. *Vide* Asnebumskit.
Hasnebumskeag Hill, near Holden. *Vide* Asnebumskit.

Hasnemesuchoth, Hassanamesitt. Mass. Bay Col. Rec. Vol. IV, p. 192.

Hassanamesitt, Grafton, Worcester Co. "At a place of small stones."

Hassanamisitt, Grafton, Worcester Co. "At a place of small stones."

Hassanamisco, Grafton, Worcester Co. "At a place of small stones."

Hassunimesut, Grafton, Worcester Co. "At a place of small stones."

Hassunnimesat, Grafton, Worcester Co. "At a place of small stones."

Hassunnek Hill, Holden. "A ledge of rocks." Eliot.

Hoanantum Hill, Charles River, Boston. *Vide* Nonantum.

Hobomoco Pond, Westborough, Worcester Co.—the Indian name for the Devil.

Hobomoc Pond, Westborough, Worcester Co.—the Indian name for the Devil.

Hobbamocke Pond, Westborough, Worcester Co.—the Indian name for the Devil.

Hoccanum, Hadley, Hampshire. "Hook-shaped."

Hoccanum, Yarmouth, Barnstable. "Hook-shaped."

Hockanum Meadows, Northampton. "Hook-shaped."

Hockanome, Hadley, Hampshire. "Hook-shaped." *Vide* Hoccanum.

Hockamock, Easton, Bristol.

Hockamock, also name of Raynham, Bristol.

Hooestunnic, same as Housatonic River, q. v.

Hoosac River, Berkshire, "mountain rock?"

Hoosichisick Lake, Milton, Norfolk Co.

Hoosicwhisick Lake, Milton, Norfolk Co.

Hosokie meadow, Lancaster, Worcester Co.

Housatenuc River, same as Housatonic, q. v., "over the mountain."

Housatonic, Stockbridge, Berkshire, "over the mountain."

Housatonnuc, Sheffield, Berkshire, "over the mountain."

Housetunack, same as Housatonic.

Housatonic River, Berkshire. "Beyond the mountain."

Humhaw Brook, in Westford. Dr. S. A. Green.

Hyanaes Village, near Barnstable. Takes name from Iyanough or Qyanough, resident chief, in 1621. H-B. of A-I. 1, 371.

Hyannis Village, near Barnstable, same as Hyanaes.

Hyannis Point, near Barnstable, same as Hyanaes.

Hyannis Harbour, near Barnstable, same as Hyanaes.

I

Igowam, same as Agawam. *New England's Prospect.* Wood, 1634.

J

Jabish River, Pelham, Hampshire Co.

Jamaica (Plain), Suffolk, "a country abounding in springs."
Jamaica Pond, Suffolk, "abundance of beavers." *Indian Bulletin,* 1867.

K

Kachewalunck Pond, Lunenburg. *Vide* Uncachewalunk.

Kamesit tract, about South Pond, Plymouth.

Katama, near Edgartown, Dukes Co.
Katama Bay, near Edgartown, Dukes Co.
Katama Point, near Edgartown, Dukes Co.

Katamawick Island, "York Records" (Me.), Vol. 3, p. 114.

Katayma Bay, Edgartown, Dukes Co. *Vide* Katama.

Katamet, part of Sandwich. *Vide* Kitteaumut and Cataumet. Gookin.

Katomucke Island, near Saconesset: one of Nashanow, or Elizabeth Islands.

Kawamasohkakannit tract, Breakheart Hill. Plym. Rec. 1, 235.

Keekamuit Neck, near Swansea, Bristol Co. *Vide* Kickemuit.

Kekamanest spring, near Swansea. Plym. Rec. Vol. 5, p. 248. 1677.

Kekamaquag, near Woodstock.

Kekamowadchaug. Derivation uncertain; possibly "quivering-hill land."

Kekamoochaug, land about Dudley, Worcester Co. Probably similar to Chaubunakungomaug.

Keketticut, same as Keticut, q. v. "On the great river." Eliot.

Kenberma, Hull, Suffolk Co.

Kenoza Lake, near Amesbury. *Vide* Canoza. "Pickerel."

Kequassagansett, Gates Pond, Berlin. *Vide* Kekamowadchaug.

Kestokas field, Nantucket. Deed, 1715.

Ketaumet, part of Sandwich. *Vide* Cataumet. Gookin.

Ketchiquut. *Vide* Keticut (near Middleborough).

Ketchiqunt (Praying station.) *Vide* Titicut. 1698.

Keticut, same as Keketticut. "On the great river." (Middleborough.)

Keuterma.

Kickemuit Neck, near Swansea, Bristol Co. *Vide* Keekamuit.

Kickemuit, South Swansea. Bristol Co.

Kisnop Creek, Berkshire, a corruption of "John Sconnoup," a Dutch settler.

Kissacook Hill, in Westford. Dr. S. A. Green.

Kitaumet. *Vide* Ketaumet. "The village of ponds."

Kitteaumut.

Kittituck, Blackstone or Nipmuck River "Great or principal river."

Konkapot River, Stockbridge, Berkshire, named for Captain John Konkapot, chief of Stockbridge Indians, 1720.

Konkapot Creek.

Konickey Cliff, Lambert's Cove.

Koskata Head, "Cross Katy;" Nantucket. Dr. Benjamin Sharp. *Vide* Coskaty.

Kowpiscowonkouett tract, near Weequancett. Plym. Rec. Vol. 1, 231.

Kunckkiunckqualluck, near Hadley. "The rolling or upset land." H. A. Wright.

Kunckquachu, Mount Toby. "High mountain." J. H. T.

Kuppowonkunok, between Hadley and Barnet. "Close bend place," or "place shut in by a bend."

Kuttatuck, Blackstone or Nipmuck River. "Great or principal river."

Kuttutuck. *Vide* Kittituck.

L

Lakeutta, Nantucket. Deed, July 6th, 1751.

Lashaway, outlet of Wickoboag Pond, West Brookfield. "Between." *Vide* Nashua and Nashaway.

M

Maanexit River, source in Worcester Co. *Vide* Mayanexit.

Maconesett Neck. Plym. Rec. Vol. IV, 131. (1666.)

Mackatoy Island, Dartmouth. Plym. Rec. Vol. VI, p. 257. (1690-1.)

Madaket Harbour, west end of Nantucket.

Madequecham. Dr. B. Sharp.
Maddequecham Pond, Nantucket.

Madaquet Harbour. Nantucket. Dr. Benjamin Sharp.

Maddequet, Nantucket.

Maddequet Harbour.

Magaehnak Village, Sudbury. Middlesex. 1678.

Magomiscock Hill, Milford; "grand-view place;" "great rock place or land."

Magumkaquag, Hopkinton, "a place of great trees."

Magunco Hill, west of Ashland, "a place of great trees."

Maguncog, Hopkinton, "a place of great trees."

Magunhog, Hopkinton, "a place of great trees."

Magunhukquok, Hopkinton, "a place of great trees."

Magunkook, Hopkinton, "a place of great trees."

Magunkaquog, Hopkinton, originally Magwonkkomuk, "place of the gift," or "granted place." H-B. of A-I. 1, 786.

Maguntaquog, modern form, "a place of great trees."

Magus Hill, Needham; named for Magus, a sachem, who owned the land.

Mahkeenac Lake, Stockbridge and Lenox.

Mahmacheckomok, Prospect Hill, Harvard. (1656). Probably named for the great Catacoonamaug sachem. H. S. Nourse.

Makamacheckamucks.

Makewaumaquest tract, Weequancett Neck, Plymouth Co. Plym. Rec. 1, 231.

Maktepos, same as Mashpee, q. v.

Mamachecomak. *Vide* Makamacheckamucks. Dr. S. A. Green. (1656.)

Mamantapett River, Rehoboth. "Wading River." Wamsutta's deed, 1666.

Mamattaquessett, or "Wading River," "north of Massapoag Pond," Norfolk. Suff. Rec. Vol. 7.

Mamre, Nantucket. Deed, 1690.

Mamwhauge, Rehoboth, Bristol Co.

Mana, Nantucket. Spotso's deed, 1692.

Manamookeagin, Abington. "The place of many beavers."
Manamooskeagin.

Manamoiett, same as Monomoy, q. v. Chatham, Cape Cod.
Manamoy.
Manamoyet.
Manamoyit.
Manomoy.
Maunamoitt.

Mananduk? "Cedar-swamp." *Vide* "Indian Names of Boston."
   Horsford, 1886.

Mananexit. *Vide* Mayanexit.

Manatacat River, Braintree. *Vide* Monatiquot.

Manaticut River, Braintree.

Manatiquot River, Braintree, "a look-out place."

Manatacat field, Braintree. Mass. Bay Col. Rec. 11, p. 40.

Manchage, Sutton, Worcester Co. *Vide* Mauchaug.
Manchaug Village, Sutton, Worcester Co.
Manchaug Pond, Sutton, Worcester Co.
Manchauge, Sutton, Worcester Co.
Manchaugas, Sutton, Worcester Co.

Mancuppic Lake, Lowell. *Vide* Mascuppic.

Maneikshun, part of Plymouth. "Black ground." Winthrop.

Manhan, Easthampton.
Manhan River, Northampton. *Vide* Minhan.

Mannamit, part of Sandwich. *Vide* Manomet. Winthrop.

Mannanpenokean Brook, running into Housatonic, at Sheffield.

Mannimeed. *Vide* Mannamit. W. Wood, 1634.

Manomet Point, Sandwich.
Manomet Hill, Sandwich.
Manomet Village, Sandwich.

Manonscussett, Sandwich, same as Scussett, q. v.

Mansikshan, Plymouth. "Blackground." *Vide* Maneikshun.

Manskusseehoank mountain, Rattlesnake mountain, Stockbridge.

Manthquohkoma Swamp, Weequancett Neck, Plymouth Co. Plym. Rec. 1, 231. *Vide* Muchquachema.

Manwhauge Plain, South Rehoboth, Bristol Co.

Maquan Lake, Hanson, Plymouth Co.

Marshpee, Falmouth, Barnstable Co. "Standing water," or "great pond." *Vide* Mashpee.

Masaksicke, Longmeadow, near Springfield. "Great meadow."
Masaksick.

Mascanomo, Manchester, Essex Co.

Mascuppic Lake, Lowell. *Vide* Mancuppic.

Mashamurket.
Mashamugget Hill, Charlton. "At the great fishing place."
Mashamugget. *Vide* Mashamoquet, Conn.
Mashgmugget.

Mashashinett tract, Weequancett Neck, Plymouth Co. Plym. Rec. 1, 231.

Mashawmut, Charlestown, Suffolk. *Vide* Mishaumut. Ogilby, 1671.

Mashepagocke Pond, near Salmon Brook, Dunstable. Mass. Bay Col. Rec., meaning probably "Bad Pond." *Vide* Massapoag.

Mashne Island, Manomet Bay.
Mashnee.

Mashomuk, Charlestown, Suffolk. *Vide* Mashawmut and Mishaumut.

Mashpee, Falmouth, Barnstable Co. "Standing water "or "great pond." *Vide* Marshpee.

Mashpoag, Sharon, Norfolk. "Great pond" or "Bad pond."

Maspenock Pond, partly in Milford, Worcester Co., "choice fishing place."

Maspenock River, Mendon, Worcester Co., "choice fishing-place."

Masquabamisk meadow, Quaboag: a bound-mark. Mass. H. S. Col. 1st, 1, 269.

Masquatuck Creek, Nantucket. Deed, 1674. *Vide* Quayz.

Mashquomah Swamp, near Assawompsett Neck. Plym. Rec. Vol. 1.

Mashquomoh Swamp, near Assawompsett Neck. Plym. Rec. Vol. 1.

Mashquttoohk (or Reod) River, Nantucket. Deed, Jan. 9, 1668.

Mashquaponitib tract, Nantucket. Deed, Jan, 9, 1668.

Masquanspust Pond, Dartmouth (Mattapoisett tract).

Masquetuck, same as Quaise, q. v.

Masqomcossick tract, Deerfield, Hampden Co. Rec. 1666.

Masquomcossick. Deerfield.

Masquomp, near Norwottock, Hampden Co. "Red rock," "red water," or "great rock."

Masquopeck tract, Nantucket. Deed, 1687.

Massabequash, Marblehead, Essex Co. (or Forest River).

Massachusetts. "At or about the great hill." J. H. T. The Rev. John Cotton, in 1708, defines Massachusetts as meaning "a hill in the form of an arrow-head," but Roger Williams says—"The Massachusetts were so-called from the Blue Hills." *Vide* Messatsoosec.

Massachusetts Village, on Massachusetts Bay. Smith, 1614. Probably one of the chief settlements of the tribe of that name. *Vide* Messatsoosec.

Massanamesit, Grafton, Worcester Co. *Vide* Hassanamesit.

Massapanoh tract, near Middleborough.

Massapoag Pond, Sharon, Groton and Lunenburg.

Massapoag Pond, Dunstable, Middlesex. "Great," or probably, "bad pond."

Massapoag Brook, Sharon, Norfolk.

Massaquockummis Brook, Brookfield, Worcester Co. *Vide* Massequockummis. Mass. H. S. Col. Vol. 1

Massassoomineuk, near Sandwich, Plymouth Co. "Place of large cranberries."

Massaugatucket River, Marshfield. "Great outlet of tidal river." *Vide* **Missaugcatucket.**

Massequockummis, Brookfield, Worcester Co. "The little marshy meadow;" or "Another brook where meadow is:" a boundmark. Mass. H. S. Col. 1st ,Vol. 1, 269. *Vide* Massaquockummis.

Masshapauge Pond, Lunenburg. *Vide* Massapoag. "Great pond" or probably "bad pond."

Massick Island, Stott's Mills, Lowell.

Massomuck, Wabaquasset village, 1700. Probably same as Mashamoquet, Massamugget, etc.

Massqunnipash Pond, Mattapoiset. *Vide* Musqunnipash.

Maswasehi Mountain, Great Barrington ; "standing up nest."

Matchapoxet Pond, near Chatham, Barnstable.

Matchapquake, near Rochester.

Matchuk meadows, Brookfield, Worcester Co. "Bad land."

Matchuk Brook, name transferred from meadows.

Matucksett Brook, near Taunton. Plym. Rec. Vol. 1, p. 242.

Mastucksett Brook; bounding a tract between Aponett and Taunton rivers.

Mattabaget, near Hadley, Hampden Co. "The rock seeks the water." H. A. Wright.

Mattacheese, Yarmouth, Barnstable. *Vide* Mattakeset.

Mattachiest, Barnstable, Barnstable Co.

Mattahquesett, Duxbury, Plymouth Co. Plym. Rec. 3, 142.

Mattakeese, part of Yarmouth, Cape Cod. Winthrop.

Mattakeesee, Yarmouth, Cape Cod.

Mattakeesett Village, Duxbury, Plymouth Co. 1685.

Mattakeset, Dukes, part of Edgartown. Winthrop.

Mattakeset, Pembroke, same as Mattacheese.

Mattaomet meadow, Hatfield, Hampshire. Same as Capowonk, q. v.

Mattaoolanick, Hatfield, Hampshire. "Land where the waters meet." H. A. Wright.

Mattapan, Dorchester, Suffolk. "A sitting down place" (for rest after carrying).

Mattapanock, Dorchester Neck, Suffolk.

Mattapoisett, Plymouth Co. *Vide* Mattabesec, Conn.

Mattapoiset. Possibly "a sitting down, or resting place after portage." 1622.

Mattapoisett River, Buzzard's Bay. "A place at a great rivulet or brook." S. G. B.

Mattapoiset Neck, Swansea.

Mattapoissett.

Mattapuyst, same as Mattapoiset, q. v. 1622.

Mattaquatcham, 1690.

Mattaquitchame Pond, Nantucket. Deed, 1692.

Mattkees, same as Mattakeese, Yarmouth.

Mattaquason, Chatham.

Mauchaug, Oxford, Worcester Co. *Vide* Manchaug. Barber, *Historical Collections,* 593.

Maugus Hill, Needham, Norfolk; same as Magus Hill, q. v.

Maunamoitt, same as Monomay, q. v.

Maunamuchoy meadow, near Mashpee. *Vide* Auntaanta. Plym. Rec.

Maunipensing, same as Monponset, q. v.

Mauswaseekhi, Monument Mountain, Berkshire. "Fisher's nest."

Mayanexit River, source in Leicester, Worcester Co. *Vide* Conn.

Meeshawn, Nauset village, Truro, Cape Cod, 1698. "Great neck."

Megansett, at Dorchester.

Megunko Hill, west of Ashland. *Vide* Magunco.

Mehtukquaaumsett, near Marion, Plymouth Co. Plym. Rec. Vol. 1, p. 231.

Memassacusett River, near Sandwich, Plymouth Co. Plym. Rec. Vol. 1, p. 134.

Memenuckquage, Swansea, Bristol Co.

Meminimisset Brook, near Brookfield, Worcester Co.

Meminimisset. H. H. Mass. Vol. 1, 265.

Menamesick Brook, New Braintree, Worcester Co. *Vide* Wenimisset.

Menameset villages. "Great Fishing-basket," or "Fishing Weir." Temple.

Menemesseg, an Indian rendezvous in 1673. *Vide* Meminimisset.

Menauhant, Falmouth, Barnstable Co.

Menchoisset, Rochester, Plymouth Co. *Vide* Monchauset.

Menemsha, Dukes Co.

Menemsha Pond, Dukes Co.

Menemsha Bight, Dukes Co.

Menomee Pond. *Vide* Monomonack, N. H. "Good grain, or seed."

Menotonomy, Arlington (West Cambridge).

Menumesse, near New Braintree, Worcester Co. Mass. H. S. Col. VI, p. 205. *Vide* Menemesseg.

Merrimack, Bradford, near Haverhill, Essex Co.

Merrimack River, Haverhill. "Rapid water," or "deep, or profound river." J. G. C.

Merrimac.

Messanegtacaneh, bound of Rehoboth. Wamsutta's deed, 1666.

Meshmuskuchtekutt tract, Weequancett Neck, Plymouth Co. Plym. Rec. 1, 231.

Messapoag, same as Massapoag, q. v.

Messatsoosec,* (Massachusetts)—Bay of "The great hill's mouth," —Charles River? *Vide* Massachusetts. Rasle.

Messatsoosec Hill, near Squantum, Suffolk. *Vide* Massachusetts Village.

Messatuag tract, near Marion, Plymouth Co. Plym. Rec. 1, 240. 1665.

---

* Refer also to "Indian Names of Boston" Horsford. 1886.

Metewemesick, near Sturbridge, Worcester Co. "Place of black earth" (Plumbago) on Quaboag River. Roger Williams and W. Tooker (1643).

Miacomet Pond, at Nantucket.

Miacomit Village, at Nantucket.

Mincomonk meadow, Hatfiefd, Hampshire; "over across land," or "land across the brook." H. A. Wright.

Mincommuck meadow, Hatfield, Hampshire.

Mingo Beach, Beverly, Essex Co. This name is said to have been that of an Indian. The Indian word means "treacherous."

Minhan Island, mouth of Manhan River, q. v. "Island." *Vide* Munhan.

Minotoquid River, Braintree. Mass. Bay Col. Rec. Vol. 1, p. 162.

Minotiquid River, Braintree. *Vide* Manatiquot, 1636.

Minnechaug, Wilbraham, Hampden Co. "Berry-land."

Minnechoag.

Minechoag Mountain, Ludlow, Hampden Co.

Miramichi Pond, near Plainville, Norfolk.

Miscoe Brook, Grafton, Worcester Co. Apparently a fragment of a name, probably the end of Hassanamisco.

Miscoe Hill, Mendon, Worcester Co.

Mishanegitaconett, Rehoboth, "near Pawtucket River." Wamsutta's deed. 1666.

Mishaum Point, Dartmouth.

Mishaum, Charles River, Norfolk. "Great Neck."

Mishawum, Charlestown, Suffolk. "Great neck."

Mishawum, Woburn, Middlesex. "Great neck."

Mishaumut, Charlestown. Wood, 1634. "Near the great neck." Deane (1822). "Near the great neck." *Vide* Mashawmut. Ogilby, 1671.

Mishawumut, Charlestown.

Misquamsqueece, near Scituate. Plym. Rec. Vol. 1, p. 96.

Misquitucket Brook, near Wareham. "Red Brook." flows into Buttermilk Bay.

Misquoc Hill, Mendon, Worcester Co. *Vide* Miscoe.

Misquoe Hill, Mendon, Worcester Co. *Vide* Miscoe.

Miskee Hill, Mendon, Worcester Co. Whitney. *Vide* Miscoe.

Mistick, Malden, Middlesex. *Vide* Mystic.

Mistik Pond, at Winchester, Middlesex. "Great River."

Mistick River, Malden and Medford. "Great River."

Missepaug, same as Massapoag, q. v.

Missaucatucket River, Marshfield, Plymouth Co. *Vide* Massaugatucket.

Missaugatucket River, Marshfield, Plymouth Co. "Great outlet of tidal river."

Missaugcatucket River, Marshfield, Plymouth Co. "Great outlet of tidal river."

Missogkonnog, Nipmuck village, Central Mass. Mass. H. S. Col. 1st, VI, 201. 1671.

Moantuhcake Hill, Washacum, Worcester Co., occurs in a deed of 1689.

Moantueake Hill, Shattuck Mss.

Mocassin Brook, Phillipston, Worcester Co., "a shoe." Probably not so named by Indians.

Moccason Brook, Phillipston, Worcester Co.

Mohawk Brook, North Brookfield, Worcester Co. Probably derived from Mohawk tribe,—the name meaning "cannibals."
Mohawk Hills, North Brookfield.

Mohawk Brook, Stockbridge, Berkshire.

Mohootset Pond, Carver, Plymouth Co. "The place of the owl."

Molpus River, Lunenburg, Worcester Co. *Vide* Mulpus.

Monadoc. Probably same as Monadnock. *Vide* N. H. W. W. Tooker. *Vide* Horsford "Indian names of Boston."

Monamesset Neck, south of Harwich, Barnstable.

Monamoyick Harbour, Orleans, Cape Cod. *Vide* Monomoy.

Monatiquot River, Braintree, Norfolk. "A look-out place." *Vide* Manatiquot.

Monchauset, Rochester, Plymouth Co. *Vide* Menchoisset.
Monchauset tract, Rochester, Plymouth Co. Winthrop.

Monechchan, Breakheart Hill, Plymouth Co. "Black bank."

Monhiggon River, runs into Quisquaset Pond, near Middleborough.

Monomac River, same as Merrimack River. H. H. Mass. Vol, 2, 343. *Vide* Monnomake, N. H.

Monomonoc Pond, Winchendon, Worcester Co. *Vide* Wonomonoc.

Monomoy Point, Chatham, Cape Cod.
Monomoy Island, Chatham, Cape Cod.
Monomoy, Chatham, Cape Cod.

Monomoy, Nantucket. Spotso's deed, 1692.

Monomoyet, same as Monomoy, q. v.
Monomoyett, same as Monomoy.
Monomoyit, same as Monomoy. *Vide* Monamoyick.

Monoosmoc Brook, Leominster, Worcester Co. "Deep brook."

Monoosnoc Hills. *Vide* Wainooset and Wahnoosnook.

Monoosuck Hills, name transferred from brook.

Moogunkawg, Hopkinton, Middlesex. Mass. H. S. Col. *Vide* Magunhog, etc.

Moonascaulton Neck, near Sandwich? Plym. Rec. Vol. 1, p. 134.

Moose Brook, Barre, Worcester Co.

Mooskupkaquant Spring, Pocasset ("Pawkeesett") Barnstable. Plym. Rec. Vol. 1, p. 241.

Monponset, Halifax, Plymouth Co.

Monponset Pond, Halifax, Plymouth Co.

Monson, Hampden Co., said to have been a favourite resort of Indians, possibly Monsoni or "Moose people."

Montague, Franklin Co. Indian territory so-named, 1753.

Monuhchogog, a former Indian village at Oxford, Worcester Co., same as Manchaug, q. v. Eliot.

Monument Mountain, Berkshire Co., of Indian origin: supposed to mark grave of first sachem.

Moona, Nantucket. Dr. B. Sharp.

Mosawquet tract, Nantucket. Deed, 1690.

Moskituash Brook, near Rehoboth, Bristol Co.

Mossonachud Hill, Leicester, Worcester. "At canoe-hill."

Mount Wachusett, Princeton, Worcester. "Mountain-place."

Moxisset? 1685. H. H. Mass. Vol. 1, p. 313. Probably derived from an Indian word signifying "a shoe" or "shoes." W. W. Tooker.

Muchquachema Swamp, Weequancett Neck, Plymouth Co. *Vide* Manthquohkoma. Plym. Rec. Vol. 1, p. 231.

Mugget Hill? Charlton, Worcester Co.

Mulpus Brook, in Shirley. Dr. S. A. Green.

Munham Island, mouth of Manhan River, q. v. Hampden Co. Rec. Wright.

Musehauge Swamp, Rutland, Worcester Co., a bound-mark. May mean "grass," or "bad land."

Musshauge Swamp, Rutland, Worcester Co.

Muschopauge, Rutland, Worcester Co. "Musk-rat Pond;" name transferred.

Muscopauge Pond, Rutland, Worcester Co. "Musk-rat Pond."

Muschopauge Pond, Rutland, Worcester Co. "Musk-rat Pond."

Muscuppic Lake, Lowell, Middlesex. *Vide* Mascuppic.

Muset Creek, Sandwich, Barnstable. Gookin.

Mushauwomuk, Boston. "A ferry," or "canoe crossing:" literally, "where there is going by boat."

Mushau-Womuk, Boston. "Canoe place," or "Ferry landing place."

Muskapasesett tract, Weequancett Neck, Plymouth Co. Plym. Rec. Vol. 1, p. 231.

Muskegat Island, Nantucket.

Muskeget, Island, Nantucket.

Muskeget Channel, Nantucket.

Musketaquid, Concord, "a grassy brook." or "the grass-grown river." Winthrop.

Musquapog. *Vide* Muschopauge.

Musquashiat Pond, near Cohasset.

Musquetequid, Concord, "a grassy brook;" or "the grass-grown river." *Vide* Musketaquid.

Musqunnipash, part of Rochester. *Vide* Masqunnipash.

Mussauwomineukonett tract, Weequancett Neck, Plymouth Co. Plym. Rec. Vol. 1, p. 231.

Musshauge Swamp, Rutland, Worcester Co., a bound-mark. May mean "grass," or "bad land." *Vide* Musehauge.

Myacomet Pond, Nantucket. Deed, April 29, 1701.

Mystic River, Medford, Middlesex.

Mystic Pond, Winchester, Middlesex. *Vide* Mistick and Mistik.

N

Naamcoyicke tract, near Eastham, Barnstable. Plym. Rec. V, p. 39. 1670. *Vide* Naumkoyick.

Naamhok, same as Naumkeag (Salem), q. v.

Naamkeak, Lowell, Middlesex. "Eel-land." J. H. T.

Nabnasset Pond, at Westfield, Hampden Co.

Nacata, near Acushnet River, Bristol Co. Mass. H. S. Col.

Nacommuck Brook, Brookfield, Worcester Co., "an enclosed point of land."

Nahant, near Lynn, Essex Co. "At the point," or, according to some, "twin islands." Nahantum was name of one of local Indian chiefs.

Nahanteau, Nahant, Essex Co. "At the point," or "twins."

Nahapassumkeck village of Mass. tribe. H-B. of A-I. Vol, 1, 316.

Nahteawamet Neck, Assawompsett, Middleborough.

Nahudset River, near Middleborough.

Nahum-keag, Salem, Essex Co. "Eel-land." J. H. T. *Vide* Naumkeag.

Nahum-keke, Salem, Essex Co. "Eel-land." J. H. T.

Nagog Pond, Littleton, Middlesex.

Nagog hill, Littleton, Middlesex.

Naggawoomcom Pond, Chauncey Pond, Westborough, Worcester Co. "Great Pond?"

Naltaug Brook, Warren, Worcester Co. Mass. H. S. Col. 1st, Vol. 1, p. 269. *Vide* Naultaug.

Nallahamcomgon Brook, Bennet Brook, Northfield, same as Natanas, q. v. Hampden Co. Records. Wright.

Namacock Neck, "near Ocinamunt Pond,"—both lying off Pottanumacutt, Cape Cod. *Vide* Naaumkoyick.

Namatakeeset, same as Mattakeeset, q. v. Mass. H. S. Col. 4th, V, p. 133., also H. H. Mass. Vol. 1, 313. Hinckley.

Namaquacket, near Little Compton. *Vide* Nanaquakett.

Namascheuck. *Vide* Namauasuck and Namasket.

Namasket, Middleborough, Plymouth Co., "a place of fish."

Namasket River, Middleborough, Plymouth Co., "a place of fish."

Namassakeese River, Pembroke, Plymouth Co.

Namatakeesett. *Vide* Wamappahesett. M. H. S. Col. 7, 2d, 278.

Namasseket. *Vide* Namasket.

Namauasuck. *Vide* Namasket.

Namecot. Plym. Rec. Vol. VI, p. 197. 1686.

Nameunkquassit, same as Namuwouxit, q. v.

Namekeake, near Chelmsford, Middlesex. Gookin.

Namkeg, Salem, Essex Co.

Namshaket, Wellfleet, Barnstable Co., "a fishing-place."

Namshaket Creek, Wellfleet, Barnstable Co., "a fishing-place."

Namskeket, Wellfleet, Barnstable Co., "a fishing-place."

Namununkset, same as Namuwouxit, q. v.

Namuwarnuksit River, same as Namuwouxit.

Namuwouxit River, near Bridgewater, Plymouth Co. Plym. Rec. Vol. 1, pp. 232-233.

Nanajcoyijcus Pond, Harvard, Worcester Co. "An Indian earthen pot" or "dry pines." *Vide* Nonacoicus.

Nanahuma, Nantucket. Dr. B. Sharp.

Nanakumas, part of Nantucket. Winthrop.

Nanahumack Neck, west end of Nantucket. Deed, 1671.

Nanamesset Island, one of Elizabeth Islands. *Vide* Nanomesett.

Nanantomqua meadows, Quaboag Pond: a bound-mark. Mass. H. S. Col. 1st, Vol. 1, p. 269.

Nanaquakett, same as Pocasset. *Vide* also Namaquacket. Nunnaquacket, Nunnacket, etc.

Nanepashemet, Marblehead Neck, so called from Nanepashemet, probably the last of the Naumkeag chief sachems.

Nanomesett Island, Gosnold, Dukes Co. *Vide* Nonamesset.

Nanomeeset Island.

Nantasco, Plymouth Co.

Nantasket, Plymouth Co. "Place of low-ebb tide."

Nantican, one of Elizabeth Islands, Dukes Co. "York Records," Me.

Nantomqua. *Vide* Nanantomqua.

Nantucket Island; appears in maps as Natocko, in 1630. *Vide* Siasconset. "At the promontory (or point of land) in a river."

Nanumackeuitt tract, east of Scituate, sold by Chickatawbut in 1668.

Naotucke, Northampton, Hampshire. *Vide* Noatucke. Norwottock and Nonotucke. Mass. Bay Col. Rec. Vol. 3, p. 360.

Naphchecoy, Nantucket. "Round Head."

Naponset, Suffolk. "He walks in his sleep?" "As he is a rapid?" "It is a good fall,"—easily passed over by canoes. *Vide* Neponset.

Naquag, extensive territory in Worcester Co., "an angle-point or corner."

Naquog, Rutland, Worcester Co.

Narraganset Hill, south-west of Plymouth.

Nasawtuck Hill, near Concord.
Nasawtuk.

Nashamoiess Village, Martha's Vineyard. 1659. Winthrop.
Nashamoless, Edgartown, Dukes. Gookin.

Nashanekammuck, Chilmark, Dukes Co.

Nashanow Islands, same as Elizabeth Islands, near Falmouth.

Nashaquitza, Nantucket.
Nashaquitsa Pond.

Nashaue-komuk, Chilmark, Martha's Vineyard. "Half-way house."

Nashawa River, at Lancaster, Worcester Co.

Nashaway, Lancaster, Worcester Co. "Between the branches of the river."

Nashawake, Lancaster, Worcester Co. "Between the branches of the river."

Nashaway River, Lancaster. *Vide* Watananock, Nashawa, etc.

Nashawannuck, near Easthampton.

Nashawog, Lancaster, Worcester Co. *Vide* Nashaway. "The land between."

Nashawena, one of Elizabeth Islands.

Nashayte, Nantucket. Dr. B. Sharp.

Nashoba Brook, Acton, Middlesex.

Nashobah, Littleton, Middlesex. (village and hill).

Nashoba Brook, in Westford. Dr. S. A. Green.

Nashoba Brook, Westfield, Hampden Co.

Nashope, same as Nashoba (Littleton.) H. H. Mass. Vol. 1, p. 156.

Nashnakemmuck, Chilmark, Dukes Co. *Vide* Nashanekam-muck.

Nashquitse, Chilmark. *Vide* Nashaquitsa.

Nashua River (arising from several sources. near Lancaster, Worcester Co.

Nashaue. *Vide* Nashaway.

Nashuakemmink. *Vide* Nashnakemmuck.

Nashwash, Lancaster, Worcester Co. *Vide* Nashaway. Winthrop.

Nasketucket, Fairhaven, Bristol Co.

Nasketucket Bay, Fairhaven, Bristol Co. Winthrop.

Nasnocomacack Village (Mass.). H-B. of A-I. Vol, 1, p. 816.

Natanas Brook, same as Nallahamcomgon, q. v. Northfield.

Natick, Middlesex Co. Derivation unsettled; some favour "a place of hills; others, "a clear place," etc. Mr. Tooker defines it as "The place of (our) search."

Naticot, near Lowell or Chelmsford: same as Namekeake. S. G. D. p. 278.

Natty Pond, Hubbardston, Worcester Co., a corruption.

Natuckett, same as Nantucket. Mass. Bay Col. Rec. Vol. IV, p. 199.

Naugus Head, Marblehead shore.

Naukeag Ponds, Ashburnham, Worcester Co., "sandy land" or "soft earth," name transferred from land.

Naukheag.

Naultaug, same as Naltaug, q. v.

Naumkeag, Salem, Essex Co. "Eel-land." J. H. T.

Naumkeek, Salem, Essex Co. "Eel-land."

Naumkuk, Salem, Essex Co. "Eel-land."

Naumkoyick Neck, west of Orleans River, Barnstable.

Naumkoyick Creek, south of Orleans River. *Vide* Naamcoyicke.

Naumosaukusset River, near Bridgewater. *Vide* Namuwouxit.

Naumox tract, west of East Pepperell road. Name of a chief. Dr. S. A. Green.

Nauset, Eastham, Cape Cod.

Nauset Beach, Eastham, Cape Cod.

Naushaun Island, Gosnold, Dukes.

Naushon Island, Gosnold, Dukes.

Nawottok, Hadley, Hampden Co. "In the middle of the river." *Vide* Norwottock, Noatucke, etc. Judd's *History of Hadley*.

Nayassett, near Agawam, Springfield, "where there is a corner." Hampden Co. Rec. H. A. Wright.

Nayyagg, near Easthampton, Hampden Co. "Point of land." or "At the point." H. A. Wright.

Nayyocossick tract, Deerfield, Hampden Co. Rec. February, 1666.

Neckatay River, near Dartmouth, Bristol Co. *Vide* Nokatay.

Neesepegesuck Ponds, Ashby, Middlesex. Name taken from brook.

Neesepegesuck Brook, "Two bond brook."

Neeseponsonset Pond, Dana, Worcester Co. "Near two ponds."

Nekatatacouek tract, Assawompsett.

Nemoset Mountain, Ashby, Middlesex: may be "near the fishing-place."

Nemunuxet River, same as Namuwouxit, q. v.

Nepassooenegg Brook, Mohawk Brook, near Hadley, Hampden Co.

Nepesoneag Brook, Mohawk Brook, Sunderland, Hampden Co. *Vide* Nepassooenegg.

Neponset, Suffolk; "He walks in his sleep?" "As he is a rapid?" "It is a good fall,"—easily passed over by canoes. *Vide* Naponset.

Nepsuchnit. Mass. Bay Col. Rec. Vol. 5, p. 97.

Nichewaug, Petersham, Worcester Co., possibly the same as Nashaway, q. v.

Nichewoag.

Nichmug River, near Grafton, Worcester Co. *Vide* Nipmuck.

Nimpanickhickanuh, Chilmark, Martha's Vineyard. "The place of thunder clefts." Mayhew.

Ninipoket, near Middleborough, Plymouth Co.

Nipmuck, Mendon, Worcester Co. "Fresh-water fishing place." J. H. T. Name of tribe in Central Mass. *Vide* "Tribes."

Nipmuck River, the Blackstone River, Worcester Co.

Nipmuck Pond, Mendon, Worcester Co.

Nipmug, same as Nipmuck.

Nipmug, name of land in vicinity of Mendon, Worcester Co.

Nipnapp River, Quinsigamond, Worcester Co.

Nipnet River, same as Nipmuck River, "a place of water;" "well watered." J. H. T.

Nippahonset Pond, Raynham, Bristol Co.

Nippahonsit.

Nippaniquet Pond, Raynham, Bristol Co. *Vide* Nippenicket.

Nippaniquit.

Nippenicket Pond, Raynham, Bristol Co., same as Nippaniquet, q. v.

Nissitisset River, Pepperell, Middlesex. *Vide* N. H.

Nissitisset Hill, Pepperell, Middlesex.

Nitchawog, Petersham, Worcester Co. "The land between." *Vide* Nashaway.

Noanat Brook, near Natick.

Noatucke, Northampton, Hampshire. *Vide* Naotucke. Norwottock and Nonotucke, Mass. Bay Col. Rec. Vol. 3, 360.

Nobadeer Pond, Nantucket.

Nobska Hill, Falmouth, Barnstable Co.

Nobscot Hill, Sudbury, Middlesex.

Nobscusset, Dennis, Cape Cod.

Nobscusset Point, Dennis, Cape Cod.

Nobsquassit, Yarmouth, Barnstable Co.

Nockege Brook, Ashburnham, Worcester Co. *Vide* Naukeag.

Nookagee Brook, Ashburnham, Worcester Co.

Nookagu Brook, Ashburnham, Worcester Co.

Nohono, at Martha's Vineyard.

Nokatay Island, near Dartmouth, Bristol Co. *Vide* Neckatay.

Nonacoicus Brook, Harvard, Worcester Co. Mass. H. S. Col. 2d, Vol. 8, 209, etc.

Nonacoicus Pond, "An earthen pot," or "dry pines."

Nonacoike. Mass. Bay Col. Rec. Vol. 4, p. 132.

Nonacoicus Brook, in Ayer; also a tract in Groton. *Vide* Coicus. Dr. S. A. Green.

Nonamesset, one of Elizabeth Islands; Gosnold, Dukes Co.

Nonandem, same as Nonantum, q. v. Mass. H. S. Col.

Nonantum, New Cambridge or Newton. "I rejoice," or "I am well-minded." J. H. T.

Nonantum Hill, Brighton, Middlesex.

Nonotuck, Northampton, Hampshire. "In the middle of the river." *Vide* Norwottock.

Nonotuck Mountain, Northampton, Hampshire. This word occurs in many forms.

Nonotucke, same as Nonotuck. Norwottock, Noatucke etc.

Nonquit.

Nonquitt, Bristol Co.

Nookagee Brook, Ashburnham, Worcester Co. *Vide* Nockege.

Noonanetum, Newton; same as Nonantum. "Rejoicing?" H. H. Mass. Vol. 1, p. 153.

Noonantomen, Newton. *Vide* Nonantum.

Noosnippi Pond. "Beaver water or pond." *Vide* Annisnippi.

Nope, Martha's Vineyard: so-called by Indians in 1642. S. G. D.

Noquochoke Lake, New Bedford.

Norwootuck, Hadley, Hampshire. Mass. Bay Col. Rec. Vol. 3, 415, 430.

Norwottock, Hadley, Hampden Co. "Far away land," H. A. Wright, or "In the middle of the river." Judd.

Norwottock Mountain, Hampden Co.

Nosset, same as Nauset. Plym. Rec.

Nosska Point, Falmouth, Barnstable. *Vide* Nobska.

Noycoy, near Hadley, Hampden Co. "It is soft" (soil). H. A. Wright.

Nubanussuck Pond, in Westford. Dr. S. A. Green.

Nucksisset, Pinguine Hole, "near Wenamett sea." · *Vide* Penguine. Plym. Rec. V. 97.

Numpaug, Edgartown, Martha's Vineyard, same as Nunnepoag, q. v.

Nunecoicus Pond, Harvard. *Vide* Nonacoicus, "an earthen pot," or "dry pines."

Nunketest River, Bridgewater, Plymouth Co.
Nunketetest River, Bridgewater, Plymouth Co.

Nunnacket, same as Pocasset Neck, q. v.
Nunnaquaquett Neck, near Little Compton. *Vide* Namaquacket.
Nunnaquoquitt Neck, Pocasset. *Vide* Namaquacket.
Nunnaquacket Neck, Pocasset.

Nunnepoag Pond, Edgartown, Martha's Vineyard. "Fresh pond."
Nunnepoag Village, Edgartown, Martha's Vineyard.

O

Occowa tract, Nantucket, 1752. *Vide* Orkawa.

Ocinamunt Pond, Eastham, Cape Cod.

Ockoocangansett Hill, Marlborough;—was an Indian planting-field.

Ocsechoxit. *Vide* Woonsechocksett.

Oggawame, part of Nantucket.

Ogguonikongquamesut, Marlborough. "Praying town." *Vide* Ockoocangansett.

Ogkoonhquonkam, same as Ogguonikongquamesut, q. v.

Ogkoontequonkamis, same as Ogguonikongquamesut, q. v. Mass. Bay Col. Rec. Vol. 4, 192.

Oguoinkongquamescit Hill. Mass. Bay Col. Rec. Vol. 4, 363.

Ohkonkemme, Tisbury, Martha's Vineyard.

Okommakemesit, Marlborough, Middlesex.

Okormaw, Nantucket. Dr. B. Sharp.

Onkatomka, one of Elizabeth Islands, Dukes Co. *Vide* Unkateme.

Onkawoom, Nantucket. Record, June 5th, 1752.

Onkowam tract, near Onset. Plymouth Co. Plym. Rec. Vol, 1, p. 240.

Onota Lake, at Pittsfield, Berkshire.

Onset, Plymouth Co.

Onset Bay, Plymouth Co.

Ontset Island, Plymouth Co.

Orkawa tract, Nantucket, 1751. *Vide* Occowa.

Osceola mountain, Richmond, Berkshire.

Oukote, Milton, Norfolk. "Place of Hills." *Vide* Unquity–quisset. H. H. Mass. 1, 156.

Oungomkos, part of tract at Wasqakage, q. v. Indian deed, 1671. "Place over across?" Wright.

Ousatunick. *Vide* Housatonic.

Ouschankamaug, Windsor, Berkshire. Winthrop.

Ouschanpamaug, Windsor, Berkshire. *Vide* Washakamaug.

P

Pacamakicke, Elizabeth Islands. "York Records," Me., Vol. 3, p. 130.

Pacatuck Brook, West Springfield, Hampden Co.   *Vide* Paucatuck.

Pachade village, near Middleborough, Cotton, 1703.   A-I. H-B. Vol 11.

Pachage Neck, between Namasket River and brook falling into Teticut River. *Vide* Ptchade.

Pachamaquast tract, near Assawompsett. Plym. Rec. Vol. 1, p. 229.

Pachaug Neck, Taunton River.   "A turning place."

Pachuach, Easthampton, Hampden Co. "Turning off place." *Vide* Pascomuck and Pasacomuck. H. A. Wright.

Pachawesit Neck, near Pocassett. Gookin.

Pacheweset, Sandwich. *Vide* Chepachewest.

Pachest tract, near Assawompsett. Plym. Rec. Vol. 1, 229.

Pachet Brook? *Vide* Pochet.

Packachoag Hill, Worcester city. Probably means "a turning place."

Packachoog Hill, Worcester city. *Vide* Packachoag and Boggachoag.

Pakachoog Hill. There are many forms of these names.

Packwake Gorge, Housatonic River, Berkshire. "Bend" or "elbow."

Pakanokick. Same as Pokanoket, q. v.

Pacummohquah Neck. Nantucket. 1662.

Pakemitt, Stoughton. *Vide* Punkapoag.

Pamanset River, Dartmouth, Bristol Co.

Pamansit River, New Bedford, Bristol Co.

Pamaquesicke, Chicopee River, Hampshire. Mass. Bay Col. Rec. 4, pt. 2, 436.

Pampaspised River, near Sandwich, Barnstable. Plym. Rec. 4, p. 3. 1661.

Pamet, Truro, Cape Cod. Eastham and Wellfleet originally included Pamet and Skeekeek. *Vide* Skeekeek.

Pamet River, Truro, Cape Cod.

Pawmet, Truro, Cape Cod. *Vide* Pamet

Pawmet River, Truro, Cape Cod. *Vide* Pamet.

Pametoopauksett Swamp. Plym. Rec. vol. 4, p. 3. 1661.

Panhanet, near Rochester, Plymouth Co.

Panoket Island, Manomet Bay. "Little land."

Panomescett Neck, near Dartmouth, Bristol Co. Plym. Rec. Vol. 6, p. 97.

Papacontucksquash, Miller's River, Montague, Hampden Co. Hampden Co. Rec. H. A. Wright.

Paquonckquamaug Lake, Belchertown, Hampshire. "At the shallow lake." H. A. Wright.

Pasacomuck, Easthampton, Hampshire. "Place where the road forks." H. A. Wright.

Pascomuck. Easthampton, Hampshire. Winthrop.

Pasamasatuate tract, near Assowompsett. Plym. Rec. vol. 1, p. 229.

Pascomansett Neck, near Dartmouth, Bristol Co.

Pascomanset River. *Vide* Pamansit.

Pascamanset River. Plym. Rec. Jud'l II, 166.

Paskesickquopoh Pond, Belchertown, Hampshire. "The branching pond." Wright.

Paskhommuck, Mount Tom, Northampton, Hampshire.

Pasocha Valley, Nantucket, Deed, July 1st, 1690.

Pasquenese, one of Elizabeth Islands, Dukes. *Vide* Penikese

Passonagesit, near Weymouth, Norfolk, "of which Chickatawbu was sachem." T. Morton, *New Canaan* pp. 106–7. 1637.

Passuntquanuncke Neck. South Sea, Barnstable Co. Plym. Rec. Vol. 4, p. 189. 1668.

Patackosi, Town Brook, Plymouth. "Narrow."

Patantatonet, near Rochester, Plymouth Co.

Patopacassett Pond, Breakheart Hill, Plymouth. Plym. Rec. Vol. 1, p. 235.

Patoompacksicke Pond and tract, Breakheart Hill, Plymouth.

Patoompawsicke Pond. *Vide* Patopacassett. Plym. Rec. Vol. 1, p. 226. (1674).

Pattaquattic Ponds, Palmer, Hampden Co.

Pattaquattic Hill.

Patucket Falls, Connecticut River, South Hadley.

Patuxet, Plymouth. "At the little falls,"

Paucatuck Brook, West Springfield, Hampden Co.

Paucomptucke, Deerfield, Franklin Co. *Vide* Pocomtuck, (1673). Mass. Bay Col. Rec. Vol. 4, part 2, 558.

Paugus, Middlesex.

Pauhunganuck Brook, Agawam, Springfield. "Land of the mill." H. A. Wright,

Pauketucke. Suffolk Co. Mass. Bay Col, Rec. Vol. 4, p. 435.

Paukokoesseke, near Wequancett Neck, Plymouth Co., Plym. Rec. Vol. 1, p. 231.

Paukopunnakuk Hill, Breakheart Hill, Plymouth. *Vide* Pockappunnakaak.

Paupakquamcook Pond. "The double pond or fishing place."

Paupogquinog Pond. *Vide* Paupasquachuke, Conn.

Pausatuke neck. Plym. Rec. Vol. 4, p. 128.

Pautage, West Brookfield, Worcester Co. "Jutting land."

Pawhikchatt River, near Marion, Plymouth Co. Plym. Rec. 1, p. 231

Pawkamauket (" King Philip's" spelling, September, 1670.) Same as Pokanoket, q. v.

Pawkeesett, same as Pocasset q. v.

Pawkunnawkutt. same as Pokanoket, q. v.

Pawmet. Truro, Barnstable. Same as Pamet, q. v.

Pawmet River, Truro, Barnstable.   Same as Pamet.

Pawpocsit, Barnstable.   *Vide* Popponessett.

Pawpoesit, Barnstable, near Mashpee.   Gookin.

Pawtucket, Chelmsford, Middlesex.

Pawtucket Falls, Lowell, on the Merrimack River.   "At the falls." J. H. T.

Pawtucket Falls, Westfield, on the Westfield River, Hampden.

Payquage, Athol, Worcester Co.   Same as Poquaig, q. v.

Payquage River, Athol, Worcester Co., same as Poquaig q. v.

Pecowsic, near Springfield, Hampden Co.

Peedee, Nantucket.   Dr. B. Sharp.

Peeskhamnet Brook, near Teticut River.

Pegan Hill, Natick.   Old map.

Peguusset, Watertown, Middlesex.   *Vide* Pigsgusset.   "Where the narrows open out."

Pekenut, Stoughton, Norfolk.   *Vide* Pakemitt and Pequimmit.

Pemamachuwatunch Mountain, Deerfield, Franklin Co.   "At the twisted mountain; Sheldon: *History of Deerfield*, Vol. 1, p. 29.

Penacook, part of Nashua River, Lancaster, "a crooked place."

Penecuck, part of Nashua River, Lancaster, "a crooked place."

Penecook, part of Nashua River, Lancaster, "a crooked place."

Penakese, one of Elizabeth Islands, Dukes.   "Sloping land." *Vide* Penikese.

Penguine Hole, near Manomet.   Mass. Bay Col. Rec. 4, p. 119 (1666).

Penikese.   *Vide* Penakese.

Penkese Island, in Monomonack Lake, Winchendcn, Worcester Co.   *Vide* Penakese, probably "sloping land."

Penticutt, Haverhill, Essex, same as Pentucket.

Pentucket, Haverhill, Essex. "At the crooked river.

Pentucket Pond, Georgetown, Essex.

Pequag, Indian name for Athol, Worcester Co. *Vide* Payquage.

Pequiog, Indian name for Athol, Worcester Co. "Cleared, or broken, land."

Pequimmit, Stoughton, Norfolk: same as Pekenut and Pakemitt, q. v. *Vide* Poquaig.

Pequod, Wayland, Middlesex.

Perquanapaqua, Lenox, Berkshire. "Lake of the still water."

Peshchameeset Island, one of Elizabeth Islands, near Falmouth. Plym. Rec. Vol. VI, p. 22 (1679).

Petapawag, Groton, Middlesex, same as Petaupauket, q. v.

Petapawage, Groton, Middlesex, "Boggy meadow," or "miry land."

Petapawage River, Groton. Mass. Bay Col. Rec. Vol. 3, 388.

Petaupauket, Groton, Middlesex.

Petho-Pogsell tract, near Wequancett Neck, Plymouth Co. Plym. Rec. Vol. 1, p. 231.

Petowamacha Hills, Hadley, Hampden Co. Rec. Wright.

Petowomuchu Hills, Hadley, Hampden.

Petowwag, Easthampton, Hampden Co. "The land from where the water flows to us." Wright.

Pewonganuck River, Northampton, Hampden Co. "Mill River." Wright.

Pewongenung River, Northampton, Hampden Co. "Mill River." Wright.

Picosick, Longmeadow. *Vide* Pecowsic.

Pigsgusset, Watertown, Middlesex. *Vide* Peguusset.

Pimesepoese River, Manomet River, Plymouth Co. 1622. "Provision rivulet." Mass. H. S. Col. 2d, Vol. 3.

Pinguine Hole, near Manomet.

Pispogutt, in Wareham, Plymouth. Gookin.

Pitchawam swamp, Granby, Hampshire.

Pitchawamache swamp, Granby, Hampshire.

Pitchuoohutt tract, near Marion, Plymouth Co. Plym. Rec. 1, p. 231.

Poatpos creek, Nantucket, 1684.

Pocasset Village, Sandwich, Barnstable Co., "where a strait widens out."

Pocasset River, Sandwich, Barnstable Co., "where a strait widens out."

Pochasuck, Westfield, Hampden Co. *Vide* Pochassic and Poyasacke, "where the narrows open out." Wright.

Pochassic Hill, at Westfield, Hampden Co. *Vide* Pochasuck.

Pochet Neck, near Orleans, Barnstable. *Vide* Pachet.

Pochet Island, near Orleans, Barnstable.

Pochik rip, off Siasconset, Nantucket. Dr. Benjamin Sharp.

Pochoboquett, near Middleborough, Plymouth Co.

Pochoke, part of tract at Wasqakage, q. v. Indian deed, 1671. Probably "a turning off place." Wright.

Pochuppunnakaak tract, Breakheart Hill, Plymouth. *Vide* Paukopunnakuk Plym. Rec. 1, p. 235.

Pocksha Pond, Lakeville, Plymouth Co.

Pocomo Head, Nantucket.

Pocopawmet village, old village of Mass. tribe.

Pocomtakuke. Mass. H. S. Col. 1st, Vol. 1, p. 148.

Pocomtuck, Deerfield, Franklin Co.

Pocomtuck Rock, Deerfield, Franklin Co.

Pocumtuck Mountain, Charlemont, Franklin Co.

Podpis, Nantucket. *Vide* Polpis. Mass. H. S. Col.

Podunk tract, North Brookfield, Worcester Co.

Podunk Pond, North Brookfield. "Place of burning." Temple.

Poekquamscutt, near Wequancett neck, Plymouth Co. Plym. Rec. Vol. 1, p. 231.

Poge, Cape, Chappaquiddick Island, Edgartown, Dukes. "Harbour," or "place of shelter."

Pohpossegoquohockegge Brook, near mouth of Concord River, Billerica.

Pohpossegosquohockegge Brook. *Vide* Popessgosquockegg. Suffolk Rec.

Poggotossuc, Endfield Plantation, east of Connecticut River. Hampden Co. Rec. A–B. 39. "A hollow."

Pojassick, Deerfield, Franklin Co. *Vide* Pochasuck.

Pokamquoh Neck, Nantucket. Deed, July 19th, 1673.

Pokanoket, Bristol. Favourite hunting-ground of King Philip. "The wood or land on the other side of the water."

Pokesset, part of Sandwich, Barnstable Co. *Vide* Pocasset. Winthrop.

Polpis, Nantucket.

Polpis Harbour, Nantucket.

Polyganset, Dartmouth, Bristol Co. *Vide* Ponaganset and Apponaganset. Douglass' *Summary*, Vol. 1, p. 403.

Pomagusset Brook, Rutland, Worcester Co.

Pomposeticut, Stow, Middlesex.

Pompositicut, Stow, Middlesex.

Pompositicut Hill, Stow, Middlesex.

Pompositicut tract, Stow, Middlesex.

Ponaganset, Dartmouth, Bristol Co.   *Vide* Polyganset and Apponaganset.

Poncammooncoe Neck, Nantucket.   *Vide* Pacummohquah.

Poniken, Lancaster, Worcester Co., possibly from Panoquin, a Narraganset who, with others, raided Lancaster, in 1675.   *Vide* Quassaponikin; may mean "the place of the ford."

Ponikin Hill, Charlton, Worcester Co.

Ponikin Village, Lancaster, Worcester Co.

Ponkapog.   *Vide* Punkapog and Punkapoag.

Ponnakin Hill.   *Vide* Poniken.

Pononokamit, Wellfleet,. Barnstable Co.   *Vide* Punonakanit.

Pontoosuc Lake, Lanesborough, Berkshire.

Pontoosuc, Pittsfield, Berkshire.

Pontoosuc River, Pittsfield, Berkshire.   "Falls on the brook."

Pontoosuc, Plainfield, Hampshire.

Pontpetsicke tract? Suff. Rec. 6, Vol. 7.

Poohookapog Pond, Sturbridge, Worcester Co.   "Cat's Pond."

Pookhookappog Pond.

Poohpoohsaug.

Poontoosuck, same as Pontoosuc, q. v.

Popessgosquockegg, at mouth of Concord River. 1671.   Mass. Bay Col. Rec. Vol. IV, part 2, p. 57.

Popoloup Island, Monomonack Lake, Winchendon, Worcester Co.

Popos Neck, near Marion. Plymouth Co.

Popponesset, part of Mashpee, Barnstable Co.   Winthrop.

Popponesset Bay, near Mashpee, Barnstable Co.

Poquaig, Athol, Worcester Co. "Cleared land," or "an open place." *Vide* Payquage, Pequag and Pequiog. J. H. T.

Poquomock Neck, east end of Nantucket. Deed, 1671. Same as Pacummoquah, q. v.

Porchcommock Pond, near Chatham, Barnstable Co.

Potcomet tract, Nantucket. *Vide* Pottacohannet.

Potanumaquut Harbour, Cape Cod. *Vide* Pottanumacutt.

Potanumsqunt Village (Nauset). Cape Cod. *Vide* Pottanumacutt.

Potebaug. *Vide* Potepaug.

Potenumacut, Eastham, Cape Cod. *Vide* Pottanumacutt.

Potepog.

Potepaug stream, Brookfield, Worcester Co.

Potepaug meadow, Brookfield, Worcester Co., "marshy or damp land",—derived from tract,—or may be a contraction for "Pootikookuppogg Indians" who lived in the neighborhood. L. B. Chase.

Potowhommet, Warwick, Franklin Co.

Pottacohannet tract, Nantucket, same as Potcomet, q. v.

Pottanumacutt Harbour, Eastham, Cape Cod.

Pottanumaquate Neck, Eastham, Cape Cod.

Pottapaug Hill, Dana, Worcester Co. Name derived from pond.

Pottapoag Pond, Dana. "A bulging out or jutting" of the water, inland.

Potapoag, near Quacumquasset Lake, Worcester Co. J. H. T.

Pottapoug Hill, Dana, Worcester Co.

Pottapoug Pond, Dana, Worcester Co.

Potumska, at New Bedford, Bristol.

Poucha Pond, near Chappaquiddick, Dukes.

Powisset, Indian village, near Dedham.

Poughkeeste, same as Pocasset, q. v.

Powwow River, Gardner, near Amesbury, Essex.

Powwow Hill, near Amesbury, Essex.

Poyassacke, near Westfield, Hampden Co. 1671. Mass. Bay Col. Rec. Vol. IV, part 2, p. 504.

Ptchade Neck. *Vide* Pachage.

Puckcommegon River, Green River, Deerfield, Hampden Co. Rec. A. 8.

Pukcommeagon River, Green River, Deerfield. Hampden Co. Rec. A. 8.

Pumpisset, part of Sandwich, Barnstable Co. Winthrop.

Pumspisset, "near Herring Pond, two miles up Manunat River." Gookin.

Punkapoag, Canton, Norfolk Co.

Punkapoag Pond, at Canton, Norfolk Co. "A spring that bubbles up from red soil," "sweet water." "Shallow pond." Gerard. *Vide* Ponkapog.

Punkapog Pond, at Canton, Norfolk Co.

Punkatasset Hill, near Concord, Middlesex. *Vide* Punkatesset.

Punkateese Hill, near Concord, Middlesex.

Punkateesit Neck, near Concord, Middlesex.

Punkatesset Hill, near Concord, Middlesex.

Punonkanit, Wellfleet, Barnstable Co. *Vide* Pononokamit.

Q

Quabaconk, same as Quaboag, Brookfield, Worcester Co., q. v. Quaboag signifies "Red-water place or pond,"Temple: or may mean land "before the pond," or "the pond before"—some other pond or tract of land. J. H. T. Many forms of this word are found in early deeds and literature. *Vide* Queboag.

Quabacutt.

Quabakonk.

Quabagud (1649).

Quabauk.

Quabbacutt.

Quabin, Greenwich, Hampshire.

Quabbin Lake, Greenwich, Hampshire. "Many waters."

Quabbin Mountain, Greenwich, Hampshire, "named after famous Indian sachem."

Quaboag, Brookfield, Worcester Co., land "before the pond," or "pond before" some other pond or tract. J. H. T. *Vide* Quabaconk.

Quaboag River, Brookfield, Worcester Co.

Quaboag Pond, Brookfield, Worcester Co. "Red-water place, or pond." Temple.

Quacumouasit Pond, near Sturbridge, Worcester Co., possibly derived from name of Quacunquasit, a sachem of Quaboag.

Quacumquasset Lake, south of Brookfield, Worcester Co. *Vide* Quacumouasit.

Quacumquaset Lake, south of Brookfield, Worcester Co.

Quaddick. *Vide* Pattaquottuck.

Quag Pond, Gardner, Worcester Co. "Pine-tree land."

Quagana Hill, at Littleton, Middlesex.

Quahmsit (Nip.). *Vide* Quamquisset, Quantisset, etc.

Quamakechett Tokopisset tract, near Assawompsett. Plym. Rec. 1, 229.

Quamquisset Harbour, at Falmouth.   *Vide* Quahmisit. S. G. D. Book 3, p. 88.

Quana, near Agawam, Springfield, Hampden Co.

Quanaconwampith, near Onset, Plymouth Co. Plym. Rec. Vol. 1, p. 240.

Quanatock, Miller's Brook, Northfield, Hampden Co.

Quanatusset, Woodstock, Praying-town.   *Vide* Conn. H. H. Mass. 1, 157.   *Vide* also, Quantisset.

Quannapowitt, Wakefield, Middlesex.

Quannapowitt Lake, Wakefield, Middlesex.

Quanesusset tract, near Mayanexit. Mass. Bay Col. Rec. V, 488 (1689).

Quanhiggin River, Mass. Bay Col. Rec. Vol. 3, p. 330.

Quanitick, Rutland, Worcester Co., a bound-mark, meaning possibly, "a tall, or long tree."

Quanpaukoessett tract, Wequancett, Plymouth Co. Plym. Rec. 1, 231.   *Vide* Paukohoesseke.

Quanset Cove, Manomet Bay, Wareham side.

Quansit Cove, Manomet Bay, Wareham side.   Winthrop.

Quansigomog, Hopkinton, Middlesex Co.   *Vide* Quinsigamond.

Quantisset, same as Quanatusset, q. v.   *Vide* also Quateseck, Quatiske, and Quatesicke.   *Vide* Conn.

Quanumpacke swamp, near Dartmouth—Mattapoiset tract. Plym. Rec. Vol. 1, p. 225 (1673).

Quapaukuk, Queensborough, Berkshire. Wright.

Quaquoountuck, near Granby, Hampshire, Hampden Co. Rec. A. 8. "The shaking-marsh creek."   H. A. Wright.

Quasapauge, Mendon, Worcester Co. "Pickerel Pond." J. H. T.

Quascacunquen, Newbury, Essex.

Quascacunquen Falls, near Byfield, Essex.

Quashnet River, at Mashpee, Barnstable Co.

Quassaponikin Hill, Lancaster, Worcester Co. *Vide* Ponikin. "At the greatest fording-place."

Quassink, Hampden Co. "Stony place." Hampden Co. Rec. Wright.

Quassink Pond, Sturbridge, Worcester Co.

Quassuck Pond, Sturbridge, Worcester Co. "The largest outlet." J. H. T.

Quateseck, Mass. Bay Col. Rec. Vol. 5, p. 426.

Quatesecke. Mass. Bay Col. Rec. Vol. 4, 2d part, pp. 357–8. *Vide* Quatissik.

Quatiske. Mass. Bay Col. Rec. Vol. 4, 2d part, p. 357.

Quatissik, Mass. Bay Col. Rec. Vol. 4, 2d part, p. 386.

Quayz, Nantucket. "Reed-land." Mass. H. S. Col.

Quaise, same as Masquetuck, q. v. Dr. Benjamin Sharp.

Queachick, Andover. *Vide* Cochichawick.

Quebaog. *Vide* Quaboag.

Queboag. *Vide* Quaboag.

Quoboag. *Vide* Quaboag.

Quenamet Neck, South Sea, Barnstable Co. Plym. Rec. Vol. 5, p. 37.

Quenaumett, near Passuntquanuncke Neck. Plym. Rec. Vol. 4, p. 189. (1668.)

Quenibeck, Rutland, Worcester Co. "Long still water." *Vide* Quanitick.

Quequechan, Fall River, Bristol Co. "Quick running water."

Quequeteant, Fall River, Bristol Co.

Quetaquas Island, near Assowompsett. Plym. Rec. V. 188. *Vide* Quittacus.

Quetaquash River, Middleborough, Plymouth Co. *Vide* Quittacus.

Quetequas Hills, Rochester, Plymouth Co. *Vide* Quittacus.

Quichechacke, Andover, Essex. *Vide* Cochickowick.

Quichichwick, Andover, Essex. *Vide* Cochickowick. *Vide Historical Sketches of Andover*; S. L. Bailey.

Quidnet, Nantucket. Dr. Benjamin Sharp.

Quillicksqu, Longmeadow, Hampden Co., "mixed, or marshy land."

Quinabaag River, Brimfield, Worcester Co., same as Quinebaug, q. v. "Long Pond."

Quinackquck, near Nonotuck, Hampden Co. "High land." Wright.

Quinapaug, same as Quinebaug, Suffolk Rec. 268, 270, 271. Vol. III, 1664.

Quinebaug River, Brimfield, Worcester Co. "Long Pond."

Quineboag River, Brimfield, Worcester Co. "Long Pond."

Quinibaug River, Brimfield, Worcester Co. Winthrop.

Qunnubbage River, Brimfield, Worcester Co. Governor Endicott, 1651.

Quinibequy River, Charles River. *Vide* Kennebec, Me. The name was transferred from Maine to Cambridge by Prince Charles,—the names being synonymous with dialectic modifications.

Quinnebeque River.

Quinobequin River, Charles River.

Quinnebequin River, Charles River.

Quinnebaug River, same as Quinebaug, q. v. "Long Pond."

Quinnepoxet River, Holden, Worcester Co.

Quinnepoxet Pond, Holden, Worcester Co. "At the little long pond."

Quinnepoxet Village, Holden, Worcester Co.

Quinobequin, at Medway, Norfolk Co.

Quinobin River, Charles River, Norfolk.

Quinshepaug, Mendon, Worcester Co. "Pickerel Pond." J.H.T. *Vide* Quasapauge and Quonshapauge.

Quinsigamond Lake, Worcester. "Long-nose (pickerel) fishing-place."

Quinsigamond, Worcester.

Quinsigamond River, Worcester.

Quisquaset Pond, near Middleborough, Plymouth Co.

Quissett Hill, Mendon, Worcester Co.

Quissitt Hill, Mendon, Worcester Co.

Quitemug Hill, Dudley, Worcester Co., name probably derived from that of John Quittamug, 1630.

Quitiquos Pond, Lakeville, Plymouth Co. *Vide* Quittacus.

Quiticus Pond, Lakeville, Plymouth Co.

Quittacus Pond, Great, Lakeville, Plymouth Co.

Quittacus Pond, Little, Lakeville, Plymouth Co.

Quittiquash Hills, Middleborough, Plymouth Co.

Quittaquas, part of Middleborough, Plymouth Co. Winthrop.

Quittaub, part of Middleborough, Plymouth Co. Winthrop, 1698.

Quittuwashett Pond, Middleborough, Plymouth Co.

Qunnubbage, same as Quinebaug, q. v. Governor Endicott, 1651.

Quivett Creek, North Brewster, Barnstable Co.

Quivett Neck, North Brewster, Barnstable Co.

Quohtauanuet tract, Wequancett, Plymouth Co. Plym. Rec. 1, p. 231.

Quonahassit, Cohasset, Norfolk. "The long rock place."

Quonackquck, near Nonotuck, Hampden Co. "High land." Hampden Co. Rec. Wright.

Quonektacut Village, Hadley, Hampden Co. 1659.

Quonshapague, Mendon, Worcester Co. "Pickerel Pond." J.H.T. *Vide* Quasapauge, Quinshepaug, etc.

Quonshapauge, Mendon.

Quosopanagon meadow, Groton, Middlesex. "On the other side of the river?"

Qunshapage. *Vide* Quonshapauge.

Qunstsipauge, original site of Mendon, Worcester Co. Mass. Bay Col. Rec. Vol. 4, 2d part, p. 341.

Qussuknashunk Rock, Breakheart Hill, Plymouth. Plym. Rec. 1, p. 235.

Quunkwattchu, Mount Toby, Hadley, Hampden Co. "High mountain."

Quyachick, Andover, Essex. *Vide* Cochichowicke. *Historical Sketches of Andover*; S. L. Bailey.

R

Rockrimmon? Springfield, Hampden Co.

S

Sabbatia Lake.

Saccarappa Pond, Oxford, Worcester Co., a name transferred from Maine.

Sachacha Pond, Nantucket.

Sackatucket, mouth of Herring River, Harwich, Barnstable Co. "The outlet of a tidal river."

Sagamore Beach, Sandwich, Barnstable Co.

Sagamore Hill, Nantasket, Plymouth Co.

Sagaquabe Island, Plymouth Harbour. Hubbard. *Vide* Sagaquash and Sagoquas.

Sagaquash Island, Plymouth Harbour.

Sagatabscot Hill, Worcester: may be "The place of hard rock."

Sagistonac Falls, Housatonic River, Berkshire. "Water splashing over the rocks."

Sagoquas Village. *Vide* Sagaquabe. H-B. of A-I. Vol. 1, p. 816. 1614.

Sagus, same as Saugus, Lynn. *New England's Prospect*; W. Wood, 1634.

Sahnchecontuckquet, at Edgartown, Dukes, 1698.
Sanchecantacket, at Edgartown, Dukes. 1698.

Sakesett Pond, near Rehoboth, Bristol Co. Plym. Rec. 1, p. 240. (1665.)

Sakonnet, Seconnet, Bristol Co.

Sanckotuck, Nantucket. Deed, Nov. 3d, 1691.

Sanctuit, same as Santuit, q. v. Winthrop.

Sankaty Head, at Nantucket.

Sankrohonk, near Nonotuck, Hampden Co., same as Sankwonk, q. v.
Sankrohoncum. "Land at the outlet." H. A. Wright.

Santuit Pond, Osterville, Barnstable Co.
Santuit, Osterville, Barnstable Co.

Sapokonist Brook, Bound Brook, Nauset (Eastham).

Saquatucket, Herring River, Harwich, Barnstable Co. "At the mouth of the tidal stream."

Saquatucket, Marshfield, Plymouth Co.

Saquish, part of Duxbury Beach. "Plenty of clams."

Sarganset River, at Taunton, Bristol Co.

Sasacacheh Village. Mass. H. S. Col.

Sasagachah Pond, Nantucket. Deed, 1745.

Sasagookapaug, Hardwick, Worcester Co. Bound-mark: possibly "Alder, or black snake, pond."

Sasaketasick, Rutland, Worcester Co. "Black-snake place." R. W.

Sassakataffick, Rutland, Worcester Co. "Black-snake place."

Sassakatassick, Rutland, Worcester Co. "Black-snake place."

Sasaquash, part of Plymouth. Winthrop.

Sasonkususett Pond, near Assowompsett. Plym. Rec. Vol. 1.

Sasonkususet Pond, bounding Nahteawamet Neck, Plymouth Co.

Sassaquin's Pond, New Bedford, Bristol Co. Probably derives its name from that of a sachem.

Satucket, East Bridgewater, Plymouth.

Satucket River, East Bridgewater, Plymouth.

Satucket territory, East Bridgewater, Plymouth.

Satucket, Harwich, Barnstable (Nauset village) 1687. "At the mouth of the tidal stream."

Satuit, Scituate, Plymouth Co. "Cold Brook." 1674.

Saucauoca tract, Nantucket. Deed, Nov. 3d. 1691.

Saughtucket, Duxbury, sold by Massassoit to Myles Standish.

Saughtuckquett, Duxbury, Plymouth Co.

Saugus, near Lynn. "The outlet," or "wet or overflown grass land."

Saugus River, Lynn, "small outlet," "extended."

Saugutagnappiepanquash tract, near Wequancett, Plymouth Co. Plym. Rec. Vol. 1, p. 231.

Saukwonk, former name of Manhan River. "At the outlet."

Sauquish, part of Plymouth. *Vide* Saquish, Sasaquash and Sayquish.

Sawahquatock, mouth of Herring River, Harwich, Barnstable Co.

Sawkatucket, mouth of Herring River. "The outlet of a tidal river."

Sawkattukett, Brewster, Barnstable Co. *Vide* Satucket.

Sawwatapskechuwas, Saw-mill Brook, Sunderland, Hampden Co.

Sayquish. *Vide* Sauquish, Saquish and Sasaquash.

Scantic Brook, near Longmeadow, Hampden Co. Hampden Co. Rec.

Scantic, near Longmeadow, Hampden Co.

Scantuck River, near Longmeadow, Hampden Co.

Scargo Lake, Dennis, Cape Cod.

Schadingmore meadows, Taunton, Bristol Co. Plym. Rec. Vol. 2, p. 100.

Scranton? *Vide* Skarnton, Praying-town.

Schenob Brook, Sheffield, Berkshire. *Vide* Schenob, Conn., said to be a corruption of Sconnoups.

Scituate, Plymouth Co. *Vide* Satuit.

Scituate Harbour, Plymouth Co.

Scook Pond, near Manomet, Plymouth Co. "The Snake."

Sconticut Neck, New Bedford harbour. "Cold Brook." *Vide* Satuit.

Sconticut Point, New Bedford harbour.

Scusset River, near Manomet, Plymouth Co.

Scusset Beach, near Manomet, Plymouth Co.

Scusset Harbour, near Manomet, Plymouth Co.

Seccasaw Village (Massachusetts tribe). H-B. of A-I. Vol. 1, p. 816. 1614.

Seconchet Village, Martha's Vineyard, Dukes. 1698.

Seconckqut Village, Chilmark, Martha's Vineyard, Dukes. Mass. H. S. Col. 1st, X, 131-132.

Seconchqut Village, Chilmark, Martha's Vineyard.

Seconet, Rehoboth, Bristol Co. Mass. H. S. Col. Vol. 1, p. 313.

Seconnet, Rehoboth, Bristol Co.   *Vide* Soghonate.

Seconesset, Falmouth (Wood's Hole).

Secouchqut, same as Seconchet, q. v.

Seeconnosset, Falmouth, Plymouth Co.   *Vide* Seconesset, etc.

Seekonk, same as Seconnet, q. v.

Seekonk River.

Secunke.

Segregansett, near Taunton, Bristol Co.

Segunesit, Nip. Village.   *Vide* Seconesset.

Seipican River, Marion, Plymouth Co. *Vide* Sippican. Mass. H.S. Col. 2d, Vol. 3.

Seketegansett, west side of Taunton River. Plym. Rec. 4, p. 5. (1661.)

Seneteconnet lands, Rehoboth.   *Vide* Seconnet. Plym. Rec. 6, p. 63. (1681.)

Senepetuit Pond, northwest corner of Rochester. "Rocky water." *Vide* Snipatuit.

Sengekontacket, north part of Tisbury, Dukes.

Sengekontakit.   Gookin.

Sepaconit, near Marion, Plymouth Co.

Sepaconnet River. *Vide* Cowasset and Sippican. "Long River."

Sepasonett, near Rochester? Plymouth Co.

Sepecan, Marion. *Vide* Sippican.

Sesachaca Pond, Nantucket. *Vide* Sachacha.

Sesuet, part of Dennis, Barnstable Co. Winthrop.

Sesuit Creek, Yarmouth, Barnstable Co. Gookin.

Sesuit Neck, Yarmouth, Barnstable Co. Gookin.

Setnessnet tract.

Shabikin land, at Harvard, Worcester Co.

Shabokin Pond, Harvard, Worcester Co. "Hell Pond."

Shabbukin Hill, near Stow, Middlesex.

Shakum Pond, Framingham, Middlesex.

Shaomet, Warwick, Franklin Co.

Shashene. *Vide* Shawsheen.

Shashin.

Shashine.

Shatterac Brook, Montgomery, Hampden Co.

Shatterack Mountain, Westfield, Hampden Co.

Shaukimmo, part of Nantucket. *Vide* Shawkemo. Winthrop.

Shaukimnes, possibly same as Shaukimmo, q. v. Mass. H. S. Col.

Shaum Neck, near Dighton, Bristol Co. "The Neck."

Shaum Neck, Cape Cod Peninsula. "The Neck." This term is applied to various necks of land on New England coast-line.

Shaume Neck, Sandwich, Barnstable Co. "The Neck."

Shaume River, Sandwich, Barnstable Co.

Shaumut. Between Fall River and New Bedford. "At the Neck."

Shaumut, at Dorchester, Suffolk.

Shawme, Sandwich, Barnstable Co. "A neck of land."

Shawkemo Hills, Nantucket.

Shawkemo Creek, Nantucket. Deed, 1673.

Shawmut, Boston, Suffolk. "At the Neck."

Shawomet, Wampanoag Village, Somerset, Bristol. "A neck of land."

Shaw-sheen, Billerica, Middlesex, said to have been derived from Sho-shanim (Sagamore Sam) a Nipmuck sachem. *Vide* Shaw-sheen River.

Shaw-sheen River, Andover, Essex. "It is smooth or glossy." Zeis: Grammar, p. 227.

Shawshene River, same as Shaw-sheen. *Vide* also Shashine, Shashin, Shashene, etc.

Shawshinock, Billerica. *Vide* Shaw-sheen.

Shenewemedy, Topsfield, Essex.

Shequocket, part of Barnstable. Winthrop.

Shewamet, Somerset, Bristol Co.

Shewamet Neck, Somerset, Bristol Co.

Shimmo Point, Nantucket.

Shimmo Shore, Nantucket. Dr. Benjamin Sharp.

Shimmoah, Indian village, Nantucket. "A spring."

Shipmuck, near Chicopee, Hampden Co.

Shockolog Pond, Uxbridge, Worcester. *Vide* Chockolog.
Shokalog.

Shonkamonke Pond, Pittsfield, Berkshire. Now Pontoosuc Lake,

Shoonkeekmoonkeek, a name for Pontoosuc Lake, q. v.

Showaluckqut, at Blackstone River, Worcester Co. "At the crotch of the river." *Vide* Wunnashowatuckqut. J. H. T.

Shuckquam, Bound Brook. Plym. Rec. Vol. 2, p. 19.

Shumuit. *Vide* Ashimuit.

Siasconset, Nantucket.

Sickcompsqu, Longmeadow, Hampden Co. "Dark-coloured rock."

Sinkunke, Rehoboth, Bristol Co. *Vide* Seekonk.

Sioug Pond, Holland, Hampden Co.

Sippican, Marion, Plymouth Co.
Sippican River, Marion, Plymouth Co.
Sippican Neck, Marion, Plymouth Co.
Sippican Harbour, Marion, Plymouth Co.

Sippigunnet River, same as Sepaconnet, q. v. "Long River."

Sippewissett, near Falmouth, Barnstable Co.

Sisickechar, Nantucket, Deed, 1682.

Skaket, Wellfleet, Barnstable. *Vide* Skeekeek and Namskeket.

Skarnton? *Vide* Scranton.

Skatehook, Westenhuck village, Berkshire. H-B. of A-I. Vol. 2.

Skauton, Nauset village, Barnstable. A-I. H-B. Vol. II, p. 40.

Skeekeek, same as Skaket, q. v.

Skenungonuck, Chicopee Falls, Hampden Co.

Skeset meadow. Plym. Rec. Judl. Vol. 2, p. 151.

Skoonkeekmoonkeek Lake, near Pittsfield.

Skug River, Andover, Essex. "Black River."

Skunkamug, Great Marshes, Barnstable.
Skunkamuk, Great Marshes, Barnstable.

Snippatuit Pond, at Rochester, Plymouth Co.

Snipatuet, at Rochester, Plymouth Co.

Sniptuett, at Rochester, Plymouth Co.

Sockanosset, Falmouth. *Vide* Succannesset. H. H. Mass. Vol. 1, p. 407.

Soewampset. *Vide* Sowampsett. *New England's Prospect.* W. Wood, 1634.

Sogkonate Point, Wood's Hole, Falmouth.

Sogkonesset, Wood's Hole, Falmouth.

Sokones, in Falmouth. Gookin.

Souhegan River, Ashburnham, Worcester Co., rises in Ashburnham Ponds and flows through Ashby to N. H. "Worn-out lands."

Sowhagon.

Sowampsett River, Lakeville, Plymouth Co. "At the red rock place?"

Sowampsett Pond, Lakeville, Plymouth Co.

Sowamsett, Lakeville, Plymouth Co.

Squabage, Brookfield, Worcester Co. *Vide* Quaboag. "Red water place." Temple.

Squabaug. Probably the original of Quaboag and its derivatives.

Squabauge.

Squabette, near Raynham. Bristol Co. Mass. H. S. Col. Vol. 3, 1810.

Squakheag, Northfield, Franklin Co. H. H. Mass. Vol. 2, p. 127. *Vide* Suckquackheag and Wussquackheag.

Squakeag, Northfield, Franklin Co.

Squam River, at Gloucester, Essex. "At the top or point of the rock."

Squam, part of Nantucket. Winthrop.

Squam Head, Nantucket.

Squamkeag, Northfield: formerly in Vermont. *Vide* Squakheag and Squakeag.

Squannacook River, at Ashby, Middlesex. *Vide* Squomacuk, R. I.

Squannacook River, at Groton, Middlesex. Probably "Place for taking salmon."

Squannacook, Townsend, Middlesex. Probably "Place for taking salmon."

Squannahonk swamp, Rehoboth. "In its present form uninterpretable." J. H. T.

Squannakonk swamp, Rehoboth.

Squannaconk swamp, Rehoboth.

Squannequeest, Manomet Bay, Plymouth Co.

Squantum, "Massachusetts Hill," near Dorchester, Suffolk. "Abundance of large rocks." *Indian Bulletin,* 1867.

Squatesit, part of Nantucket. Winthrop.

Squaw Pond, at Wilmington, Middlesex.

Squawbally, south part of Raynham, Bristol Co.

Squenatock Brook, Northfield, Franklin Co. *Vide* Quanatock.

Squibnocket, Gayhead, Dukes.

Squibnocket Pond, Gayhead, Dukes.

Squibnocket Point, Gayhead, Dukes.

Squibnocket Beach, Gayhead, Dukes.

Squipnocket, Gayhead, Dukes.

Stannox, Sherborne, Middlesex, a corruption.

Statehook, part of Sheffield, Berkshire. Winthrop. *Vide* Skatehook.

Statuckquett, near Bound Brook.

Succannesset, Falmouth, Barnstable.

Succonet. *Vide* Seconet and Sogkonate.

Succonusset, same as Succannesset and Sokones.   Winthrop.

Suchow, near Granby, Hampshire. "Dark-colored earth." H. A. Wright.

Suckquackheag, Northfield, Franklin Co., same as Squakeag.

Suckquakege. Mass. Bay Col. Rec. Vol. 4, part 2, p. 436. (1669.)

Suet Neck, Yarmouth. Mass. H. S. Col. Vol. 1.   Gookin.

Sumpauge Pond, Rutland, Worcester Co. "Beaver's Pond"? A bound-mark.

Sunmuckquommuck, near Hadley, Hampden Co. "At the rough country." H. A. Wright.

Sunsicke Hills, West Mountain, Deerfield. Hampden Co. Rec. 1666.

Suntaug Lake, Lynnfield, Essex.

Swampscott, near Lynn, Essex. "At the red rock;"—"Broken waters," or "Pleasant water place."

T

Taconic Mountain, Mt. Washington, Berkshire. "Forest," or "wilderness." *Vide* Taghkannuc and Taughkaughnick, Conn.

Tadmucke, near Chelmsford, Middlesex. Mass. Bay Col. Rec. Vol. 3.

Tadmuck, a brook and meadow, in Westford.   Dr. S. A. Green.

Talaquya, Attleborough, Bristol Co. "Place of small trees or bushes."

Talaquega, Attleborough, Bristol Co.

Talhanio, part of Chilmark, Martha's Vineyard. Gookin. 1659.

Tanquesque, Sturbridge, Worcester Co.

Tantiusque land, Sturbridge, Worcester Co. Probably derived from name of Tantiquieson, a resident sachem.

Tantousque land.

Tashmoo Pond, West Chop Beach, Dukes.

Tashmuit, part of Truro, Barnstable. Winthrop.

Tashnuc Spring, Tisbury, Dukes.

Tassacauset Neck, near Seconnet, Bristol Co. Plym. Rec. Vol. 4, p. 152.

Tassacust Neck, near Seconnet, Bristol Co. Plym. Rec. Vol. 4, p. 128.

Tataesset Hill, near the Cascade, Worcester Co.

Tataeset Hill, Worcester. "At the place of the rocking-stone."

Tatassit, Quinsigamond, Worcester. "At the place of the shaking stone." *Vide* Tataesset.

Tatnuck, same as Tatnit, q. v.

Tatnit Hill, Worcester. "At the hill,"—the name having evidently been transferred to the brook and the village.

Tatnit Brook, Worcester.

Tatnit village, Worcester.

Tatumasket, "beyond Mendon," Worcester. H. H. Mass. Vol. 1, p. 267, 1675.

Taugkannuc Mountain, same as Taconic. q. v.

Taughkaughnick Mountain, same as Taconic, q. v.

Tuakonnock Mountain, same as Taconic, q. v.

Taupaugoh River, Williams River, near Housatonic, Berkshire.

Taupoowaumsett Pond, Wequancett Neck, Plymouth Co. Plym. Rec. Vol. 1, p. 231.

Tausakaust, same as Tassacust, q. v.

Tautauchanekanesseke tract, Pocasset. Plym. Rec. Vol. 1, p. 241.

Tautemco, Nantucket. Dr. B. Sharp.

Tawtemco, Nantucket. Dr. B. Sharp.

Tchobacco, same as Chebacco and Chobocco, q. v.

Teaticket. *Vide* Titicut.

Tecticut, Taunton, Bristol Co. "On the great river." J. H. T.

Tehticut River, Marlborough, Middlesex. "On the great river."

Tehticut River, Taunton, Bristol Co., same as Tecticut.

Teightaquid, part of Marlborough, Middlesex, same as Titicut, q. v.

Teikiming, part of Tisbury, Dukes. *Vide* Tockiming.

Tekoa mountain? Montgomery, Hampden Co.

Tetankimmo, part of Nantucket. Winthrop.
Tetaukimmo, part of Nantucket. Mass. H. S. Col.

Tetehquet, same as Titicut, q. v.
Tetiquet, same as Tecticut, q. v.

Tihonet Village, Wareham, Plymouth Co.
Tionet Point, Wareham, Plymouth Co. "Place of the crane."

Tisquaquin Pond, Middleborough, Plymouth Co.

Tist, name of territory at Dedham, Norfolk. Nason.
Tiot, name of territory at Dedham, Norfolk.

Titicut Village, North Middleborough, Plymouth. "At the great river."

Titicut, Taunton, Bristol Co., same as Tecticut, q. v.

Titicut, near Bridgewater, Plymouth Co.,—the supposed source of the Taunton River.

Tittituck, a name of Blackstone River. *Vide* Kuttatuck and Kitticut. "Great or principal river." J. H. T.

Tockiming, Tisbury, Dukes. *Vide* Teikiming.

Tohkecommumwachuck, or ake, tract. "Nipmuck country." Suffolk Rec. 463, Vol. 5, 1668.

Tokopissett tract, near Assowompsett. *Vide* Quamakechett.

Tomhaummucke, Sackett's Brook, Westfield. Hampden Co. Rec. A, 49.

Tomhomock. Wright.

Tomholissick tract, Deerfield. Hampden Co. Rec. Feb. 24th, 1666.

Toneset Neck, southeast of Town Cove, Orleans, Barnstable.

Tonisset, Fall River, Bristol Co.

Tonset, Tisbury, Dukes.

Topeent, ancient Mass. village. H-B. of A-I. Vol. 1, p. 816.

Totant, ancient Mass. village, near Boston? H-B. of A-I. Vol. 1, p. 816. 1614.

Totapoag. Mass. village. A-I. H-B. Vol. II.

Totheet, Mass. village near Boston. A-I. H-B. Vol. II.

Totoket Hill, New Bedford, same as Titicut, "on the great river."

Touissett Neck, Swansea, Bristol Co. *Vide* Towansett.

Towansett Neck, Swansea, Bristol Co, same as Touissett.

Toweset Neck, Swansea, Bristol Co, same as Towansett.

Towtaid, Leicester, Worcester Co. "At the open field?"

Towunucksett River, Fort River, near Hadley, Hampden Co. "Place of the ford."

Trabagazanda, Gloucester, Essex.

Tuckanuck, Nantucket. Deed, June 20th, 1672.
Tuckernuc Island, Nantucket. "Loaf of Bread." Dr. B. Sharp.

Tugmemug, at or near Cohasset, Norfolk.

Tuppatuett, runs into Quittuwashett Pond, at Middleborough.
    "River's mouth."

Tuscomanest tract, Middleborough, Plymouth Co.

Tuttomnest Neck, near Nauset (Eastham), Barnstable.

U

Uckatimes, little island or neck: one of Elizabeth Islands, near
    Falmouth. Plym. Rec. Vol. 6, p. 22.

Ueques, Hardwick bound-mark, Worcester Co., probably "at the
    end." *Vide* Wequaes.

Umpachene River, New Marlborough, Berkshire: name derived
    from that of an Indian sachem.

Umpachene Falls, New Marlborough, Berkshire.

Umpame, an Indian name of Plymouth. *Church's History*;
    S. G. Drake.

Umsquattanack, Endfield plantation,—east side of Connecticut
    River. "Beaver-dam place." H. A. Wright.

Uncachewalunk Pond, Lunenburg or Bolton? Worcester Co.

Uncanoonuc Hill, at Lowell, Middlesex.

Uncataquisset, Milton, Norfolk.
Uncataquissit, Milton, Norfolk.

Uncatena, one of Elizabeth Islands, Gosnold, Dukes.

Uncheckcathaton Pond, near Fitchburg, Worcester Co.

Unkachewatunk Pond, same as Uncachewalunk, q. v.

Unkateme, one of Elizabeth Islands, Dukes. *Vide* Uncatena.

Unkety Brook, at Dunstable, Middlesex.

Unquetenassett Brook, Groton. Dr. S. A. Green.

Unquetenorset Brook, Groton. Dr. S. A. Green.

Unquity-Quisset, Milton, Norfolk. *Vide* Uncataquisset.

Unquety. "Place of hills." *Vide* Oukote.

Unquomouk Hill, Haydenville, Hampshire.

Unquomonk Hill, Haydenville, Hampshire.

Unsatuit tract, Wequancett Neck, Plymouth Co. Plym. Rec. Vol. 1, p. 231.

Unset Cove, Manomet Bay, Wareham side. *Vide* Onset.

Usquaiok River, near Agawam, Springfield. "The end of the land." Hampden Co. Rec. Wright.

Ussowwack tract, Deerfield, Franklin, Hampden Co. Rec. (1666.)

V

Vckatimes, little island, one of Elizabeth Islands, Gosnold, Dukes, near Falmouth. Plym. Rec. 6, p. 22. *Vide* Uckatimes.

W

Waashacum Ponds, Sterling, Worcester. "The Sea." R. W;— or "Springs." Parsons.

Waban, Middlesex, near Newton.

Waban Lake, Needham, Norfolk.

Wabquissit, now included in Conn: formerly in Worcester Co. *Vide* Conn. (Praying-town.)

Wacagasaneps tract, near Assowampsett. Plym. Rec. Vol. 1, p. 229.

Wacatuc, Uxbridge, Worcester Co. *Vide* Wacuntug and Wacuntuck.

Wacantuck, same as Wacatuc.

Wachamaucutt Neck, Rehoboth. Plym. Rec. Vol. V, p. 139.

Wachemscussett Brook, near Assowompsett. Plym. Rec. Vol. V, p. 98. (1672.)

Wachpusk tract, near Assowampsett, Plymouth Co.

Wachusett Mountain, Princeton, Worcester Co., "near the mountain."

Wachuset, Princeton, Worcester Co., "near the mountain."

Wachusett Brook, Princeton, Worcester Co., "near the mountain."

Wachuset Brook, Plympton, Plymouth Co., "near the mountain."

Wachusett Pond, Westminster, Worcester Co., "near the mountain."

Wacobske Cliff, Chilmark. *Vide* Wesquabsqu.

Wacosta, near Onset, Mass.?

Wacuntug, Uxbridge, Worcester Co. *Vide* Wacatuc and Wacantuck. "At the bend of the river."

Wacuntuck, Nip. village, 1674.

Wadchusett. *Vide* Wachusett.

Waddaquodduck Mountain, Worcester Co. *Vide* Wataquadock.

Waeuntug, Uxbridge, Worcester Co., same as Wacuntug, q. v.

Wagumquacog, Hopkinton, Middlesex. Eliot.

Wagutuquab Pond, Nantucket. Mass. H. S. Col.

Wahconah Falls, Windsor, Berkshire.

Wahnoosnook. *Vide* Monoosnoc, Monoosuck and Wainooset H. H. Mass. Vol. 1, 407.

Wainooset hills and stream, near Leominster. *Vide* Monoosuck. H. H. Mass. Vol. 1, 407.

Wakoquet, near Mashpee, Barnstable. *Vide* Waquoit. Gookin.

Wallum Pond, Douglas, Worcester Co. *Vide* Alum Pond. "Fox Pond?" S. G. B.

Wallamanumps Falls, on Chicopee River, Hampden Co. "Red standing-rocks."

Wallamanumpscook, Rutland, Worcester Co., a bound-mark.

Wamappahesett, same as Namatakeesett, q. v. M. H. S. Col. 7, 2d, 278.

Wamesit, Tewksbury, Lowell, Middlesex Co. The praying-town of the Pawtuckets, and once the redman's capital-seat, signifying "the place for all."

Wammasquid, part of Nantucket. Winthrop.

Wampaketatekam tract, near Assowompsett. Plym. Rec. Vol. 1, p. 229.

Wampoketatekam tract, near Assowompsett.

Wampum, Wrentham, Norfolk Co.

Wampum's Rock, near Wrentham, Norfolk Co. Formerly occupied by an Indian family, named Wampum, as a residence.

Wamsutta, near New Bedford, Bristol Co.

Wamsutta, near Attleborough, Bristol Co.

Wanacomet Pond, Nantucket. Dr. Benjamin Sharp.

Wanascohockett, near Rochester, Plymouth Co.

Wancenquag Brook, near Carver, Plymouth Co.   *Vide* Wankinquog.

Wanchatopeck Pond, Princeton, Worcester.

Wanchatopick, land at Naquag, Rutland. Bound-mark in Deed, 1686.

Wankinco River, Wareham, Plymouth Co.

Wankinquog Brook, between Plymouth and Carver.

Wankonquag, probable name of Cedar-swamp, near Carver.

Wannamoiset Neck, Swansea, Bristol Co.

Wannamoiset, Swansea, Bristol Co.

Wannasquam, Nantucket: more commonly called Squam, q. v. 1751.

Wanomchouck Ponds, Worcester Co.

Wanommock Ponds, Worcester Co. Possibly "Grape country."

Wannacomet, Nantucket. "Pond-field."   Dr. B. Sharp.

Wanomoycet Neck.   *Vide* Wannamoiset.

Wanoosnoc, Fitchburg.   *Vide* Monoosnoc.

Wanottimyes River, Newton, Middlesex.

Wanpawcutt Pond, Black Sachem's Pond?

Wansaquatomska River, near Rehoboth? Plym. Rec. Vol. 1, p. 240.

Wapoompauksett, Muddy Hole. Plym. Rec. Vol. 4, p. 3.

Wapowage. This name has been erroneously attributed by several authorities to Milford, Worcester Co.   *Vide* Wapowage, Conn.

Waqua Point, Edgartown, Martha's Vineyard.   *Vide* Wasque.

Waquettaquage Pond, west end of Nantucket. Deed, 1671.

Waquittaquay Pond, west end of Nantucket.

Waquoid Bay, Barnstable.

Waquoit Village, Barnstable, 1674.

Waquompohchukoit tract, near Marion, Plymouth. Plym. Rec. 1, 231.

Waqutuquaib. *Vide* Waquettaquage. Dr. B. Sharp.

Waranoco, Westfield, Hampden Co. *Vide* Worronoco, Worrin-oke, etc. Trumbull says the meaning of these words is not definitely settled.

Warranocke.

Waranoke.

Warunlug, Uxbridge. *Vide* Waeuntug. M. H. S. Col. 3d series.

Wasapskotock, Prospect Hill, Westfield, Hampden Co. "The shining-rock land." H. A. Wright.

Washaame Hill, near Nashaway. Mass. Bay Col. Rec. Vol. 5, p. 39. (1675.)

Washacum Ponds, East and West Stirling, Worcester Co. *Vide* Waashacum.

Washakamaug Village, Farm Pond, Framingham. *Vide* Ous-chaukamaug.

Washqua outlet, Mattakeeset Bay, Martha's Vineyard.

Wasqakage, Northfield, Franklin Co. *Vide* Wussquackheag. Indian Deed, 1671.

Wasque, same as Waqua Point, q. v.

Wassapacoasett tract, near Dartmouth,—"Mattapoisett tract." Plym. Rec. Vol. 1, p. 225. (1673.)

Watananock River, same as Nashua River, Worcester Co. Probably derived from land. "Land about the hill." (1673.) Mass. Bay Col. Rec. Vol. 4, 2d part, p. 569. J. H. T.

Wataqua, Nashua River, Lancaster, Worcester Co. The original name of Nashua River, meaning "Pickerel." J. G. C.

Wataquadock Hill, Brimfield. Worcester Co.

Wataquadock Brook, Brimfield, Worcester Co. *Vide* Wadda-quodduck.

Wataquadock Pond, Brimfield, Worcester Co. Name derived from hill, also name of Brook and Hill, Bolton, Worcester Co.

Watatick Mountain, Great, northeast of Gardner, Worcester Co·

Watatick Mountain, Little.

Watatick Pond, Ashburnham, Worcester Co. "Wigwam Brook."

Watchemoquit Cove, Seekonk, Bristol Co.

Watchemoquet Neck, Seekonk, Bristol Co.

Watchusecic Hill, Uxbridge.   Probably a diminutive of Wachu-set,—meaning "At the little hill."

Watchymoquett, same as Watchemoquit, q. v. Plym. Rec. Vol. 2, p. 55.

Watuppa Pond, at Fall River, Bristol Co.

Watuppa, Fall River, Bristol Co.

Waubansconcett, in original petition for grant of Groton, etc. Dr. S. A. Green.

Waumpanicksepoot, Green River, Berkshire.

Waunashqua, Nantucket.

Wauphaneeskitt tract, Wequancett Neck, Plymouth Co. Plym. Rec. Vol. 1, p. 231.

Waushaccum. *Vide* Washacum. Deed, Feb. 26th, 1751, same as Wannasquam and Squam, q. v.

Wauwinet, at Nantucket.   Named from local chief.

Wawayoutat, Wareham, Plymouth Co. 1674. Gookin.

Wawaytick Creek, near Menemsha Pond, Dukes.

Waweypounshag, bound of Rehoboth. Wamsutta's deed, 1666.

Wawona, at Swansea, Bristol Co.

Waymessick, Chelmsford, Middlesex.   Mass. H. S. Col.

Weakpocoinke Hill, near Black Bank, Breakheart Hill, Plymouth. Plym. Rec. Vol. 1, p. 226. (1674.)

Weeketuket Brook, Jones River, Plymouth. "Little wading-place."

Weckwannuck, Sugar-loaf Brook, Whately. Hampden Co. Rec. A. 133.

Wecoachett meadow, near Sandwich, Barnstable.

Wecobaug. *Vide* Wickabaug.

Weecodnoy, Nantucket.   Dr. B. Sharp.

Weechagaskas, Weymouth, Norfolk.   *Vide* Wessagusset. Gookin.

Weecaasuck Island, same as Weikeset, q. v.   Suffolk Rec. 307, 308, Vol. IV, 1659.

Weepecket Island, one of Elizabeth Islands, Gosnold, Dukes.
Wepecket. *Vide* Woepecket.

Weequancett Neck, near Namasket River, Plymouth Co. S. G.D.
Wequancett Neck, near Namasket River, Plymouth Co.

Weequakut, Barnstable.   *Vide* Waquoit.

Weesquobs, in Sandwich, Barnstable.
Weesquobs River, Sandwich, Barnstable, same as Penguine River.
Wesquobs Village, Sandwich, Barnstable, "eel-fishing by torch-light"? 1674.

Weeset Neck, near Pochet, Orleans, Barnstable.

Weeweder Pond, Nantucket.   Deed, 1690.

Weikeset Island, in Merrimack River, near Lowell.   Mass. Bay Col. Rec. Vol. 5, p. 430.

Wekapekatonnuc Hill, Leicester, Worcester Co., bound-mark.

Wembemesiscook, Hardwick, Worcester Co. *Vide* Wowbeme-siscook.

Wcnatukset Stream, Monponset, Plymouth Co.

Wenatukset, Plympton, Plymouth Co.

Wenatuxet Village, Plympton, Plymouth Co.

Wenatuxet River, Plympton, Plymouth Co. *Vide* Winnatuck-set.

Wenaumet, Pocasset, Barnstable Co.

Wenaumet Neck, Pocasset, Barnstable Co.

Wenimesset, New Braintree, Worcester Co. Winthrop.

Wennuchus Lake, at Lynn, Essex.

Wenunckemis tract, Suff. Rec. 289, Vol. XII, 1682.

Wenunkeynnj Brook, between Medfield and Natick. (1665.) Mass. Bay Col. Rec. Vol. 4, 2d part, 285.

Wepecket. *Vide* Weepecket.

Wepoiset, Swansea, Bristol Co.

Wequaes, Hardwick, Worcester Co., a bound-mark (1686). "The end." *Vide* Ueques.

Wequanhausicke Pond, Agawam, Springfield, Hampden Co. R. A–B, 21.

Wequaquet Lake, Centreville, Barnstable.

Wequaset tract, Chatham, Barnstable Co.

Wequettayyag, Northampton, Hampden Co. "Land at the bays." H. A. Wright.

Wequittayyag.

Weronoke, Westfield, Hampden Co. *Vide* Woronack, etc.

Wesappicoasett tract, at Mattapoisett, Plymouth Co.

Wescussauco, Newbury (old town), Essex.

Weshake'm, same as Nashaway, Worcester Co.

Weshakim, same as Nashaway, Worcester Co.   Gookin.

Weshamon Woods, near Lancaster, Worcester Co.

Wesko Harbour, east end of Nantucket.   "The White Stone."
Indian Bulletin, 1867.

Wesco tract, east end of Nantucket.

Wesquabsqu Cliffs, Martha's Vineyard.

Wessacucon, Newbury (old town).   Mass. Bay Col. Rec. Vol. 1,
p. 146.

Wessacumcon.

Wessaguscus, Weymouth, Norfolk.   *Vide* Wessagusset. S. G. D.

Wessaguscusset, Weymouth, Norfolk.   *Vide* Wessagusset.
S. G. D.

Wessaquscus, Weymouth, Norfolk.   *Vide* Wessagusset.

Wessagusset, Weymouth, Norfolk.

Westenchuck, Stockbridge, Berkshire.

Westenhuck Village, Stockbridge, Berkshire.

Westgostoqua, North Yarmouth.   Winthrop.

Wetuset, probably same as Wachuset.   *Church's History,* p. 69.

Weweantic River, Wareham, Plymouth Co.

Weweantit River, Wareham, Plymouth Co.

Wewensett tract, near Rochester, Plymouth Co. "Young bucks"?

Whakepee, near Mashpee, Barnstable.

Whipsufferage, Plantation land at Marlborough, Worcester Co.

Whipsuppenicke, Marlborough, Worcester Co.

Whipsuppenicks, Marlborough, Worcester Co.   *Vide* Wippsufferage.

Wiano, near Osterville, Barnstable.

Wicabaug Pond, West Brookfield, Worcester Co. "At the good pond." Wright. *Vide* Wickabaug.

Wichaguscusset, Weymouth. *Vide* Wessagusset. Winthrop.

Wickabaug, Indian village, West Brookfield, Worcester Co. "At the end of the pond," or "sweet water?" J. H. T.

Wickaboag, same as Wickabaug, q. v.

Wickapicket Brook, Sterling, Worcester Co. Probably derived from the name of Wickapema, a sachem, meaning "Basswood." J. H. T.

Wickasauke Island, in the Merrimack, near Lowell.

Wickasaukee. *Vide* Wicosuck.

Wickasuck Island, at Tyngsborough, Middlesex, same as Wicosuck, q. v.

Wickataquay Pond, Martha's Vineyard;—communicates by a narrow opening with Vineyard Haven. J. H. T.

Wicosuck, same as Wickasauke and Wickasuck.

Wigwam Hill, Mendon, Worcester Co. *Vide* Weataug, Conn.

Wigwam Hill, Lake Quinsigamond, Worcester Co. *Vide* Weataug, Conn.

Wikapokotownow, Leicester, Worcester Co. *Vide* Wekapekatonnuc.

Wikkabaug, same as Wickabaug, q. v.

Willimansett, Chicopee, Hampden Co.

Winechoag Mountain, at Ludlow, Hampden Co.

Wingaersheek, Gloucester, Essex.

Wingaersheek Beach, Annisquam, Gloucester.

Winimisset, New Braintree, Worcester Co. *Vide* Wenimesset. Winthrop.

Winotemies River, Newton, Middlesex, same as **Wanottimyes**, q. v.

Winnatuckset Stream, Plympton, Plymouth Co.

Winnatuckset Village, Plympton, Plymouth Co. *Vide* **Winne-tuxet.**

Winneashimut, Chelsea, Suffolk. "At the good spring." *Vide* **Winnisimmet.**

Winneasquam, Swampscott, Essex. "Beautiful water-place."

Winneconnet Pond, Norton, Bristol Co.

Winnecunnet Pond, Norton, Bristol Co. "Beautiful place of pines."

Winnemoiset, Braintree, Mass.

Winnetsemet, Chelsea, Suffolk. *Vide* **Winnisimmet.**

Winnetuckquett tract, near Bridgewater. Plym. Rec. Vol. 2, p. 68.

Winnetuxet River, near Bridgewater. *Vide* **Winnatuckset.**

Winnikenni Hill, near Amesbury, Essex.

Winnimisset Brook, New Braintree, Worcester Co., flowing into Ware River. *Vide* **Meminimisset.**

Winnipesiekett, Swampscott, Essex.

Winnisimmet, Chelsea, Suffolk.

Winisemit, Chelsea, "Swamp Hill"? *Indian Bulletin*, 1867. (Winnisimet was sachem of Chelsea.) *Vide* **Winneashimut.**

Wippsufferage. *Vide* **Whipsufferage.**

Wisconemuck Pond, "north of Merrimack River." Mass. Bay Col. Rec. 4, 2d part, 289. Probably near Amherst or Milford N. H. *Vide* N. H.

Wishoea Pond, near Satucket, Bridgewater, Plymouth Co, Plym. Rec. Vol. 5, p. 109. (1672-3.)

Wissatinnewag Village, on Conn. River, Central Mass. 1663. H-B. A-I. Vol. 2.

Wnahtukook, great meadow, at Stockbridge, Berkshire, same as Wnogquetookoke, q. v.

Wnogquetookoke, great meadow, at Stockbridge, Berkshire.

Woepecket Island, one of Elizabeth Islands. *Vide* Wepecket.

Wokonocob River, Pocasset. Plym. Rec. Vol. 1, p. 239.

Wollomonopoag, Wrentham, Dedham, Norfolk.
Wollompauge, Wrentham, Dedham, Norfolk.

Wombemesiscook, land at Hardwick, Worcester Co.
Wombemesisecook, land at Hardwick, Worcester Co.
Wombemsicunck, land at Hardwick, Worcester Co.
Wombomesscock, land at Hardwick, Worcester Co.

Wonammanitt tract, Wequancett Neck, Plymouth Co. Plym. Rec. Vol. 1, p. 231.

Wonasquam Village, Cape Ann. *Vide* Annisquam.

Wonasquatucket Stream, Rochester, Plymouth Co. "At the end of the tidal river."

Wonchesix. *Vide* Woonksechocksett.

Wonckcompss Brook, Hatfield, Hampden Co. Rec.

Wonconquake River, near Sippican (Marion), Plymouth Co.
Wonickcomquake River. Plym. Rec. Judl. *Vide* Wonquaquake.

Wonketopick, same as Wanchatopick, q. v.

Wonksacoxet, same as Woonksechocksett. "Near the place of the foxes?"

Wonomonoc Pond, Winchendon, Worcester Co. *Vide* Monomonoc.

Wonquaquake River, near Marion, Plymouth Co. Plym. Rec. Vol. 2, pp. 258, 271.

Wonnashquoom, Nantucket, same as Wannasquam, q. v.

Wonnesquam, Cape Ann. *Vide* Annisquam. "At the end of the peninsula"? J. H. T.

Woolummonuppoque, Dedham, Norfolk.

Woonksechocksett, land at Sterling, Worcester Co. *Vide* Chocksett, also Wonksacoxet.

Wooqutcakoospa tract, near Mashpee, Barnstable Co.

Woronoack, Westfield, Hampden Co. "The winding land." Wright.

Woronoco, Westfield, Hampden Co.

Worrinoke River, Westfield, Hampden Co.

Worronoco, Westfield, Hampden Co. "The country with windings." H. A. Wright.

Woruntuck, Mass. village. A-I. H-B. Vol. II.

Wosqakag, same as Wasqakage, q. v. Indian Deed, Jan. 6th, 1671. H. A. Wright.

Wullamanick Hill, Brookfield, Worcester Co. "Red Paint Country."

Wunnaqueckset, near Hadley, Hampden Co. "At the end place." Wright.

Wunnashowatuckqut, Blackstone River, Worcester Co. "At the crotch of the river." J. H. T.

Wusquiawwag tract, Deerfield. Hampden Co. Rec. Feb. 24th, 1666.

Wussquackheag, Northfield, Franklin Co., same as Squaheag, q.v.

Wyben? Westfield, Hampden Co.

Wyoma, North Saugus, Lynn, Essex.

Wyoma Lake, near Lynn.

Wyngaersheek, Gloucester, Essex. *Vide* Wingaersheek.

Y

Yokum, Richmond, Berkshire.

Yokun Pond, Becket, Berkshire.   Name derived from that of Indian chief.

Yokun Brook, Lenox, Berkshire.

Yokun's Seat, mountain in Lenox. Berkshire.

Yowunckhomuck, Hatfield, Hampden Co.   Hampden Co. Rec. A. 11.

LIST OF MASSACHUSETTS, OR NATICK, INDIAN WORDS*

Pomantam, author of life.

Annogssue Kesuk, the starry heavens.

Puhpeeg, a trumpet or music.

Oskon, a hide.

Weween, a horn.

Tumunk, a beaver.

Wonkussis, a fox.

Poopohs, a cat.

Poohpoohsuog, cats.

Attuk, a deer.

Annum, a dog

Mishannek, a squirrel.

Nattoshqussuog, wolves.

Psukses, a bird.

Wompohtuk, a goose.

Sesep, a duck.

Monish, a hen.

Nampash, a cock.

Wunnuppoh, a wing.

Kongkont, a crow.

Mesonk, the hair.

Muskesuk, the eye.

Mutchon, a nose.

Wou, an egg.

Wowonash, eggs.

Woddish, a nest.

Wosketomp, a man.

Mittamwossis or

Eshqua, a woman.

Nonkup asuh, a boy.

Wusskennin, a girl.

Wuskenin or

Nunkomp, a young man.

Wunnechanyog, children.

Kehchius or

Nukkone wosk, an old man.

Papequanne mohtunt, an old woman.

Wosketompoo, manhood.

Mohhog, a body.

Keteahogkau, a soul.

Wawænin, a witness.

Wuttotimein, a nation.

Missinnin, people.

Muppuhkukquaset, a toe.

Oapwas, the hip.

Mehquau, the thigh.

* Selected from Josiah Cottons "Vocabulary of Mass: Language."

Wonnunou, a cheek.

Anwunnissue muskesuk, a most handsome face.

Missustoon, a lip.

Menan, a tongue.

Meepit, a tooth.

Muttoon, the mouth.

Missitteippeg, the neck.

Mittik, a shoulder.

Muppuhkukquanitch, a finger.

Muppuhkuk, the head.

Muskonontip, a skull.

Meesk, the elbow.

Menutcheg, the hand.

Unninuhkoe, the right hand.

Menatche, the left hand.

Missippuskunnicheg, wrists.

Mohpanneg, the breast.

Uppoochenou, the bosom.

Muppuskq, the back.

Mukkuttuk, the knee.

Muhkont, the leg.

Misseet, the foot.

Namas, a fish.

Ashap, a net.

Uhquon, a hook.

Anishamog, codfish.

Chunkoo, or

Apwonnah, an oyster.

Kopposh, a sturgeon.

Pakonnotam, a haddock.

Mishqushkou, a trout.

Mogquon, the heel.

Mishoon, the chin.

Nannumiyeu, the north.

Sowaniyeu, the south.

Wekeneankquat, warm weather

Tohkoi, cold weather.

Sonkqueu, cold.

Mehpit, an arm.

Wapan, wind.

Wutchepwoshe wittin, east wind.

Neepanon, a shower.

Nehchippag, dew.

Koon, snow.

Missegkon, hail.

Nimbau, thunder.

Ukkitshamun, lightning.

Wadchu, a mountain.

Oonouwohkoai, a valley.

Quequan, an earthquake.

Womonittuonk, love.

Sekeneadtuonk, hatred.

Penomp, a maiden.

Mittumwussis, a wife.

Wuttookasin, a mother.

Wunnamonien, a son.

Uhpuoonkash and

Uhpooonk, pipes and tobacco.

Kesukod, a day.

Nepauz, a month.

Upposhpishaonk nepaz, sun-rise.

Oowayaonk nepaz, sun-set.

Nompoae, morning.

Sukkissuog, clams.

Wawamek, a dress.

Onkqueekhoo, a hat.

Muttassash, stockings.

Mohkissonash, shoes.

Uppeshou, a flower.

Kossepeshou, a rose or lily

Appuonk, a chair or stool.

Ohkuke, a kettle.

Appui, a bed.

Pinaquet, a blanket.

Wasaquonanetick, a light or candle.

Ohhomaquesuuk, a needle or pin.

Pohsequae, noon.

Nukkon, night.

Pasukkodtummo, a year.

Assannitta, Sunday.

Nesikquinshunk, Monday.

Nishikquinishonk, Tuesday.

Yauquinishonk, Wednesday.

Napannatashikquinishonk, Thursday.

Nequttatashikquinishonk, Friday.

Nesasuktahsheke sukod, Saturday.

Nequt.	1.
Nees,	2.
Nish,	3.
Yau,	4.
Napanna,	5.
Nequtta,	6.
Nesasuk,	7.
Shwosuk,	8.
Paskoogot,	9.
Piog,	10.
Piog nabo nequt,	11.
Piog nabo nees,	12.

Manunussish ut pepenauonat ketomp: qut anue manunussish osoowunnonat noh-hannoo mahche pepenauonche.

Translation.

Be slow in choosing a friend, but slower in changing him when thou hast chosen.

Tohneit wunnetooe pomantaman kusseeppee keteaonk tapi: tohneit mat wunnetooe keteaan koosomee seeppee pomantam.

Translation.

If thou hast lived well, thou hast lived long enough: if thou hast not lived well, thou hast lived too long.

LIST OF THE PRINCIPAL AMERICAN-INDIAN TRIBES, REPRESENTING THE ABORIGINES OF NEW ENGLAND

Aberginians, a term used by the Massachusetts settlers to designate the Indian tribes to the northward. H-B. A-I. Vol. 1, p. 1.

Abnaki or Abenaqui,—"men of the east" or "Eastland." They constituted an Algonquian confederacy centered in the state of Maine which subsequently overflowed into the northern section of New Hampshire. They are said to have consisted, linguistically, of all the tribes occupying the East or Northeast shore of America. The term was first applied to the Indians of Nova Scotia. They occupied mainly the whole of the country between the Piscataqua and Penobscot rivers. *Vide* Introduction.

Agawams. The word Agawam is said to mean "a fishing station" or "fish-curing place." Two or three places in Mass. were so-called; the Indians resident at Wareham, Plymouth Co. were Wampanoags, in 1620— and those living at Ipswich, in Essex Co. (probably Mass. Indians or Nipmucks) at the same time, were both known as Agawams.

Algonkins or Algonquians, were the most widely extended of all North Americans Indians, their territory stretching along the Atlantic coast from Labrador to Pamlico Sound and westward from Newfoundland to the Rocky mountains. Their various tribes, linguistically affiliated, spoke innumerable dialects. The meaning of the word is "on the other side" (of the river), or "at the place of spearing eels, and other fish,"—from the bow of canoe. H-B. A-I. Vol ., p. 38.

Amoskeags or Namaoskeags (Nipmucks of New Hampshire) were situated at the Amoskeag Falls on the Merrimack, in the vicinity of Manchester. The name has been defined as meaning the term "a fishing place for alewives."

Anasagunticooks or Arosagunticooks. This tribe was a branch of the Abnaki nation and dwelt about the sources of the Androscoggin river.

Armouchiquois. *Vide* Malecites.

Aucociscos, a branch of the Abnaki. They occupied territory between Saco and the Androscoggin river. The meaning of is given as signifying "a crane "or "a heron."

Canibas. *Vide* Kanibas.

Etchemin. This tribe is now considered to have been a sub-group of the Abnaki confederacy, speaking the same language, but a different dialect and to have included the Passamaquoddy and Malecite. They are said to have extended from the Penobscot to the St. Croix river as far as St. John. Later they resided in the neighborhood of Passamaquoddy river. The meaning of the term has been interpreted as "Canoe-men."

Hammonassets, a tribe in Connecticut, resided in the neighborhood of Clinton and Killingworth. Sebequanash, or "The man who weeps," was their head sachem.

Hassanamissits, a tribe of Nipmucks, occupied the site of Grafton, Mass.; they embraced Christianity in 1660.

Kanibas, a branch of the Abnaki, who occupied both sides of the Kennebec river, Maine.

Machemoodus, a small tribe, probably a fragment of the Wangunks, situated near East Haddam, Conn. Much superstition prevailed among them owing to mysterious noises proceeding from the adjacent hill known as "Mount Tom," and here the Indians, as an early writer says:—"drove a prodigious trade at worshipping the devil!"

Mahicans, Mohicanders or Monahiganeucks, an Algonquian tribe extending from Esopus to Albany on the banks of the Hudson, in 1610. The term means "a wolf " or "wolves." This tribe must not be confounded with the Mohawks, who were of a different nation and language, or with the Mohegans of Connecticut, q. v.

Malecites or Marachites (Marechites), a branch of the Abnaki occupying the St. John river, New Brunswick. The term is said by Chamberlain to mean "broken-talkers." They were called "Armouchiquois" by the French Missionaries and their closest linguistic affinity is with the Passamaquoddy dialect. They are also known as "Maliseets."

Maquas. *Vide* Mohawks.

Marechites. *Vide* Malecites.

Mashpees or Marshpees, Wampanoags in and about the township of Mashpee, Barnstable Co., Mass. The name is derived from Indian words signifying "great pool." In 1660 Mashpee served as a reservation for the Christian Indians of the vicinity known as South Sea Indians. They intermarried with negroes freely and still later, with Hessians. In 1832 the mixed race numbered 332.

Massacos, a branch of the Tunxis, q. v. Known also as Simsburys, Conn.

Massachusetts, had dominion, for the most part over the eastern territory adjacent to Massachusetts Bay. The limitations of their territory, which was probably much more extensive, have not been accurately defined. About 1617 this tribe was decimated by a pestilence and their territory seems to have been divided amongst the Nipmucks, Narragansetts and other tribes. *Vide* Introduction.

Mattakees, a small tribe in Nauset territory (Mattakeset, Yarmouth, Barnstable Co., Mass.), probably subject to the Wampanoags. *Vide* Gookin, Mass. H. S. Col. 1st. Vol. 1, 148 (1806).

Micmacs. "The earliest aborigines of the American continent to to come in contact with Europeans." They constituted a large and influential tribe occupying mainly Nova Scotia, Prince

Edward's Island, Cape Breton, the northern part of New Brunswick and parts of Newfoundland. The French designated them as "Souriquois," and their name is supposed to signify "our allies." *Vide* Introduction.

Mohawks, the most eastern of "The Five Nations,"—Huron-Iroquois,—at one time, perhaps, the most powerful Indian confederacy that ever existed. The Mohawk villages occupied mainly the valleys of the Mohawk river. N. Y., and their name signifies "eaters of live meat"(*i. e.* bear). In the literature of New England they are designated by many names of which probably the most frequent are "Maquas" and "Mohocks."

Mohegans, a clan or division of the Pequots, fostered and ruled by Uncas after the death of Sassacus in 1637. Their original locality was on the Thames river, Conn., in the northern part of New London Co., but, as the results of subsequent conquests their territory became very much extended. The meaning of the name according to Trumbull, is "a wolf." *Vide* Introduction.

Montauks. This tribe formerly occupied the east end of Long Island, where they were at the head of thirteen tribes living there. They were closely related to the Indians of Massachusetts and of Connecticut. Although gradually decreasing, they preserved their hereditary chieftancy until 1875, when David Pharoah, their last king died.

Nashuas or Nashaways. These consisted of a tribe of Nipmucks who dwelt on or about the mouth of the Nashua river.

Naticks, a name applied to the Indians resident in and about the town of Natick in Middlesex, Mass. They belonged to the Mass: tribe and it was amongst them that the Rev. John Eliot established the first Indian Church in New England, in 1660. The meaning of the term is uncertain (Rider). *Vide* Mass. Place-Names.

Narragansets, a term derived from "the little island of Nahiganset" at the head of Point Judith Pond. (S. S. Rider.) *Vide Proper Names* in this volume. The territory occupied by this distinguished tribe, according to Gookin, extended about 30 or 40 miles from Sekunk and Narraganset Bay, including Rhode Island and other islands in that Bay. The Narragansets were separated from the Pequots by the Pawcatuck river. The most flourishing period in the history of this great tribe was in 1642 and under the chieftancy of Canonicus.

Nausets. This comparatively small tribe was located about the territory now known as Eastham in Plymouth Co. The Nausets appear to have been subject to the Wampanoags and they were the first tribe of Indians encountered by the Pilgrims after their arrival. (1620.)

Netops, these constituted a small tribe among the Sogkonates, q. v.

Newichewannocks. This tribe belonged to the Abnaki nation, and although their principal seat was on the Cocheco river, near Dover, N. H., they were intimately associated with the tribes occupying the Piscataqua river and its branches, Maine.

Niantics or Nehantics, these were really a tribe or branch of the Narragansets and resided principally at Wekapaug now Westerly in Rhode Island. Their chief sachem was Ninigret, a cousin of Miantunnomoh. A section of this tribe resided in Connecticut and were known as Western Niantics, q. v. The term means "At a point of land on a (tidal) river or estuary." J. H. T.

Nipmucks or Nipnets; this tribe dwelt mainly in the eastern interior of Massachusetts occupying many of the lakes and rivers. Their exact limits have not been defined but they must have been very extensive, as there is proof that their boundaries reached as far as Boston on the east, as far south as the northern portion of Rhode Island,—westward as far as Bennington in Vermont and as far north as Concord, New Hampshire. *Vide* Introduction.

Norridgewocks,—a branch of the Abnaki, who dwelt upon the Kennebec river.

Onagounges, a term applied by Mohawks to all the eastern Indians.

Pawtuckets, a branch of the Nipmucks, were located in Middlesex Co. on the territory now occupied by the town of Chelmsford, on the Merrimac river.

Passamaquoddies; this tribe was a branch of the Abnaki, being also known as Openangos. They were situated on the Schoodic river and on the waters and inlets of Passamaquoddy Bay, Me. The term means "pollock-plenty place."

Paugussetts, a tribe situated in and about Stratford, Huntington, and the surrounding townships in Connecticut. The territories of this clan stretched fifteen or eighteen miles along the coast and its number appears to have been very considerable. The Wepawaugs, who occupied the east bank of the Housatonic, opposite the Paugussetts, evidently belonged to the same people. *Vide* Wepawaugs.

Pennacooks: these formed part of the great Nipmuck confederacy occupying the banks of the Merrimack river in Massachusetts and New Hampshire under the valiant and judicious leadership of the great Passaconaway. The Pennacooks resided on the territory now occupied by the city of Concord, N. H., and the jurisdiction of Passaconaway extended at least, as far as Chelmsford, Middlesex Co., Mass., in a southerly direction, where the Pawtuckets were established.

Penobscots,—a branch of the Abnaki,—dwelt on an island in the Penobscot river, a few miles from Bangor, Maine.

Pequakets (Abnaki), occupied territory on the Saco river, especially about its sources, up to 1725, when they were exterminated by the English.

Pequots. This large and distinguished tribe was in all probability, originally descended from the Mahicans in New York State. Their territory extended from the Niantic river on the west to ten miles east of Paucatuck river, which divides Connecticut from Rhode Island (R. W.). Sassacus, their great sachem, had, it is said, no less than 26 sachems under him, when they were at their zenith. They were vanquished in 1637. *Vide* Introduction.

Podunks, a tribe occupying East Windsor and East Hartford, Conn. They appear to have been closely connected with the Poquonnuc Indians on the other side of the Connecticut river.

Pokanokets. *Vide* Wampanoags.

Potatucks, a Connecticut clan, who were located north-west of the Paugussetts, "within the limits of Newtown, Southbury, Woodbury, and some other townships," of whom little has been recorded, beyond the sales of their lands.

Quinnipiacs, the aboriginal inhabitants of New Haven, East Haven, Branford, and Guilford. Their territory extended from the Wepapaugs, on the west, to the Hammonassetts of Clinton and Killingworth, on the east. Their last sachem was said to have died about 1730. (De Forest.)

Ramapoos, a name by which the Ridgefield Indians of Conn. were known. They formed part of a tribe formerly existing at Greenwich, Stamford, and Norwalk and early in the 18th century they were ruled by a sachem named Catoonah. In 1708 they sold their lands and disbanded.

River Indians was a term applied to several tribes: thus the Mohicans or Mahicans dwelling south of the Iroquois, down the north side of the Hudson river, N. Y., were so denominated, as were also some clans of the Nipmucks, and, at an early period, all the Indians dwelling on the banks of the Connecticut River etc.

Rockomekos ("great corn-land") was the name of a tribe which constituted a branch of the Pequakets whose head-quarters were at Fryeburg, Me. They were exterminated by small-pox about the middle of the 18th century. Rockomeko was situated in the neighborhood of Canton, Oxford Co., Me.

Sokokis or Sockhigones, was the name of a branch of the Abnaki, settled on or about the Saco river, Me.

Souhegans, a branch of the New Hampshire Nipmucks, who lived upon the Souhegan river, and upon both banks of the Merrimack, above and below the mouth of the Souhegan.

Stockbridge or Housatonic Indians.   These were located in Stockbridge ("Housatonic") Berkshire Co., Mass. and were principally known in connection with the missionary efforts made amongst them during many years, beginning from 1734.   They subsequently removed to a town in Oneida Co., New York, after the Revolution, where they remained 34 years and still later, departed for Wisconsin.

Sogkonates, a tribe of which Awashonks was squaw-sachem. She exercised her sachemdom at or near the mouth of Seconnet river, and on the point then known as Sogkonate, later as Seconnet, and which now including the town of Little Compton, R. I., extends from Fogland ferry to the sea, in length between 7 and 8 miles.   Here dwelt the Sogkonate tribe who, as far as can be judged, were numerous and who contributed to the downfall of Philip, although history contains few, if any, details of their achievements.

Tarratines or Tarrateens, a term used by Pilgrims and early settlers to denote the Abnaki; but while modern authorities seem inclined to accept this view there is doubt as to the aboriginal source of this term.   After the exodus of the main body of the Abnaki to Canada the term Tarratines was applied to the Indians occupying the Penobscot river from source to sea and the contiguous territories.

Tunxis or Sepous, resided on the Farmington river, eight or ten miles west of the Connecticut.   At an early period they were subject to Sequassen, the sachem who sold Hartford to the English, and they probably formed a part of the great confederacy which had formerly occupied the Connecticut valley.

Wabinga, a section of the Mahicans who were known also as River Indians. *Vide* River Indians. They had their dwellings "between the west branch of Delaware and Hudson's river, from Kittatinney ridge down to the Ɪriton." Jefferson's Notes, 308.

Wamesits were Nipmucks located near Wamesit Falls on the Concord river near its confluence with the Merrimack, in the neighborhood of the present city of Lowell, the site of which was the central point of the lands of the Pawtucket tribe. At Wamesit in 1674, there were 15 families of "Praying Indians", but a year or so later they were all disbanded or destroyed during Philip's war, and their lands were seized by their rapacious white conquerors.

Wampanoags or Pokanokets, the subjects of "Good Massassoit", and subsequently of his son, Philip, constituted the third greatest nation of the Indians in New England when it was settled by the English. The term has been defined by Dr. Trumbull. as meaning *Eastlanders*, and their territory included what is now called Bristol County (Rhode Island) Tiverton, Little Compton and the entire southern part of Plymouth Colony. The principal residence of the great chiefs of the Wampanoags was called Mount Hope, now included in Bristol, R. I. Pokanoket represented the dominion of the Wampanoags.

Wangunks, a Connecticut tribe of some importance, whose territories stretched from below Hartford to a considerable distance south of Middletown. Their chief sachem was named Sowheag.

Wawenocks, Waweenocks or Weweenocks constituted one of the main divisions of the Abnaki, and were said to be the immediate subjects of the great Bashaba or supreme ruler who resided in the vicinity of Pemaquid. Their settlement extended from the east of Sagadahoc to St. George river, but after the death of the Bashaba in 1615, they located on the west side of the Sheepscot river, near the lower falls. They were known as "the ancient regal race."

Wepawaugs; these lived on the eastern bank of the Housatonic river, Conn. and were probably identical with the Paugussetts, q. v.

Western Niantics, a sub-division of the Niantics, whose territory extended from Connecticut river eastward along the shore to Niantic river.

Zoquageers, a branch of the Abnaki who resided on the eastern shore of Lake Champlain.

Many other sub-ordinate tribes are mentioned in the early literature of New England, but they were comparatively unimportant. The following list will serve as an example:—

Accominta, a small tribe formerly dwelling in a village named Agamenticus near the site of York, Maine. They have been regarded as belonging to the Abnaki (Smith) but more probably as Pennacooks (Schoolcraft). H-B. A-I. Vol. 1, p. 8.

Amaseconti or Aumissoukanti, an Abnaki tribe which occupied territory near Farmington Falls, Sandy River, Me.

Capawocks, Mass. Indians, settled at Martha's Vineyard.

Cushnocs, of Augusta, Me.; one of the Kanibas clans.

Manisses, the aborigines of Block Island, R. I.

Medoctee, a small Abnaki tribe, 1721, on St. John River, New Brunswick.

Missiassik, formerly living on Missisquoi River, Vermont, and probably "wanderers" related to Sokokis or Pequakki.

Muanbissik, unidentified, but mentioned as included among the Abnaki in a return sent to Governor of New England in 1721. H-B. of A-I. Vol. 1, p. 954.

Nawaas, an unidentified tribe dwelling between Scantic and Podunk, Conn. A-I. H-B. Vol. 2, p. 46.

Pocomtocks, Mass. tribe, resident at Deerfield.

Quaboags, Nipmucks, in neighborhood of Brookfield, Mass.

Taconnets, of Waterville, Me.—a clan of the Norridgewocks.

Winnepesaukees, in the vicinity of Lake Winnepesaukee, N. H.

Wunnashowatuckoogs, a Nipmuck clan in Worcester Co., Mass. subject to Canonicus.

BIBLIOGRAPHICAL LIST OF PRINCIPAL WORKS CONSULTED

History of New England. Dr. Palfrey.

History of Massachusetts Bay. Hutchinson, 2 vols., 1795.

History of Narraganset. Hon. E. R. Potter.

History of Rhode Island. Hon. S. G. Arnold.

History of Vermont. Thompson.

History of Massachusetts. G. L. Austin.

History of New England. Governor Winthrop.

History of New Hampshire. Belknap.

History of Maine, 2 vols. Dr. Williamson.

Ancient Dominion of Maine. Rufus King Sewall, 1859.

History of Vermont. Dr. R. Williams, 2 vols, 1809.

Ogilby's "America," 1671.

"History of New York", Broadhead.

"History of Indians of Connecticut." De Forest, 1851.

Dr. A. Gallatin's "Vocabularies."

"Observations on Mohegan Language." Jonathan Edwards.

"Biography and History of Indians of North America." S. G. Drake, 1857.

Vocabulary of Mass. Indian Language. Josiah Cotton.

Heckewelder's "On Indian Names." Trans. Am. Philos. Soc. No. 4, 361.

"Indian Geographical Names," Trumbull; Conn. H. S. Col. Vol. 2, 1870.

"Indian Names of Places in Connecticut." Dr. J. H. Trumbull.

"Indians of New Hampshire." Hon. J. G. Crawford, 1898.

Gazateer of Massachusetts. Elias Nason, 1874.

"Indian Names of Places in Rhode Island."   Dr. Usher Parsons, 1861.

"Key to the Indian Language."   Roger Williams; Mass. H. S. Co.

Church's "Indian Wars."   Edited by Drake, 1845.

"Early History of Vermont."   L. Wilbur, 1899.

History of Vermont.   Carpenter and Arthur, 1854.

History of Rhode Island.   Peterson, 1853.

History of Vermont.   Francis Chase.

Hayward's Gazateer of New Hampshire, 1849.

Farmer and Moore's Gazateer of New Hampshire, 1823.

"History of Manchester" (N. H.)   C. E. Potter, 1856.

"History of Hadley."   Judd.

"History of West Brookfield."   Temple.

Gazateer of Maine.   Varney.

"Woods and Lakes of Maine."   Lucius L. Hubbard, 1884.

Gazateer of Maine.   Hayward.

Natick Dictionary.   Dr. J. H. Trumbull.

"Indian Local Names."   S. G. Boyd, 1885.

Bartlett's Historical Records of Mass. and Conn.

"Historical Description of Boston."   Dr. Shurtleff.

"History and Antiquities of Boston."   Drake.

History of Andover, Mass.   Abiel Abbot, 1829.

"Historical Sketches of Andover," Mass.   Miss Bailey.

"Indian Names of Boston."etc.   E. N. Horsford, 1886.

"Indian Names in Salisbury, Conn."   J. W. Sanford, 1899.

Historical Sketch of Salisbury, Conn.   Malcolm S. Rudd, 1899.

"Bibliotheca Glottica."   Trübner, 1858.

"The Bibliography of Vermont."   Gilman, 1897.

Gazateer of Vermont.   Thompson.

"Indian Bulletin," for 1867.

Report of Am. Soc. for promoting the civilization of Indian tribes.   Greenleaf, 1823.

"Algic Researches." Schoolcraft, 1839.

Historical Gazateer of Vermont, Hemenway, 5 vols.

"Hand-book of the American Indians." Vol. I. and II. Bureau of Ethnology.

"The Lands of Rhode Island." Sidney S. Rider.

Pilling's "Bibliography of Algonquin Indians."

"Language of the Abnaquies." Willis.

"New England's Prospect." W. Wood, 1634.

"Bibliography of Local History of Mass." J. Colbourn.

"History of Augusta." J. W. North, 1870.

"History of Barrington." T. W. Bicknell, 1898.

"History of Westerly." Rev. F. Denison, 1878.

Place-Names of Providence Plantation (XVIIth century). Clarence S. Brigham, 1903.

"Names of Towns in Mass." W. H. Whitmore.

"History of Lynn." Newhall, 1865.

"Old Paths and Legends of New England." K. M. Abbott, 1903.

Johnston's Gazateer.

"On Plymouth Rock." S. Adams Drake, 1904.

Sketch of Dover, N. H. J. C. Stevens, 1833.

History of Concord, N. H. Nathaniel Bouton, 1856.

"Landmarks of Ancient Dover." Miss M. P. Thompson, 1892.

History of Concord, N. H. Edited by J. O. Lyford, 2 Vols. 1896.

"Purchas' Pilgrimage" (from Hakluyt Papers) 1628.

Reed's "History of Bath." 1894.

"Groton during the Indian Wars." Hon. S. A. Green, M.D., LL.D., 1883.

"Indian Deeds." H. A. Wright.

Mass. Bay Colonial Records.

Plymouth Records.

History of Derby. Orcutt.

Providence Early Records.

Registry of Deeds, Providence.

New Hampshire Records.

History of Waterbury. Rev. Dr. Anderson.

Collected Records of Conn.

Conn. Records of Lands, etc.

Mass. Hist. Soc. Collections.

Mass. Hist. Soc. Proceedings.

Maine Hist. Soc. Collections.

Maine Register.

R. I. Historical Soc. Collections.

Numerous Encyclopædias, Maps, Deeds, Bulletins of Ethnological Bureau and of Geological Survey, many hundreds of Local Histories, etc., etc.

Also by R.A. Douglas-Lithgow:

Native American Place Names
of Connecticut

Native American Place Names
of Rhode Island

Native American Place Names
of Maine, New Hampshire, & Vermont

For more information about these and
other fine American reprints, contact

Applewood Books
P.O. Box 365
Bedford, MA 01730